# Making It Through

## Bosnian Survivors Share Stories of Trauma, Transcendence, and Truth

Demaris S. Wehr, PhD
Foreword by Polly Young-Eisendrath, PhD

CHIRON PUBLICATIONS • ASHEVILLE, NORTH CAROLINA

By the Same Author

*Jung and Feminism: Liberating Archetypes*

## *Praise for* Making It Through

*"In this beautifully written book, Demaris Wehr presents a brief history of the war in Bosnia, illuminating a moment in human history that some people prefer to forget. But as Wehr explains, forgetting does not contribute to forgiveness, which is the only thing that will help humanity create a different, more loving future. Readers will be captivated by the guiding image of the book, the centerpost around which eight stories of survival revolve. Each survivor describes a different centerpost, the one thing that helped them make it through and return home, including family, optimism, faith, duty, and more. The final message of the book is that each of us must find our own centerpost in turbulent, chaotic times in order to stand, with the author, for the possibility of peace. By reading these stories, you too will see 'what the best of humanity can do under the worst of circumstances.'"*

— Elizabeth Èowyn Nelson, PhD, author of *The Art of Inquiry* and *Psyche's Knife*

*"I followed the news about the Bosnian conflict when it was happening, but I couldn't touch the pain. The hope that Demaris Wehr has found through the voices of these narrators is palpable. Her choice of the centerpost image brings a clear focus to that place in the heart where fear can be transformed into courage. And her Jungian insights help, as well. Like this quote, 'There is no lunacy people under the domination of an archetype will not fall prey to.' We in America now live in presence of the Trumpian archetype, where truth is adumbrated. Sometimes even the memory of what truth was is erased.* Making It Through *is a powerful reminder of how*

*we can meet this kind of adversity with courage and forgiveness."*
— Robert A. Jonas, editor of *The Essential Henri Nouwen*

*"This book about one of the darkest moments of Western history since the last world war is paradoxically an extraordinary book of hope. It is a book of hope because it shows how very ordinary people who could have been you or me managed to rise above hate and the total disruption of their lives. Here are eight people whom the author interviewed and who had been through sheer hell. The eight narrators made it through by healing others and remaining connected with the deepest essence of their being and learning to forgive what would to many seem unforgivable. Authentic forgiveness is first and foremost a gift one makes to oneself, which is why it enables one to remain whole. This book of interviews enriched by Demaris Wehr's profound insights will appeal to both professionals in many fields as well as the layperson."*
— Pierre Pradervand, author of *The Gentle Art of Blessing*

*"A book of immeasurable heart and practical wisdom that can help each of us identify our own 'centerpost' and 'way home.' These inspiring stories will appeal to people of all religious and political persuasions.* Making It Through *shows how to survive and thrive in an increasingly chaotic and difficult world—a treasure map for our times."*
— Michael Dowd, author of *Thank God for Evolution*

*"Demaris Wehr's deeply inspiring book explores a paradox: In listening to survivors of the Bosnian War, she is struck not only by the searing trauma of the conflict, but also by the remarkable forms of resilience that arose in the face of it. Indeed, many survivors tell her of strengthened capacities for compassion, love, and hope. Through a series of thought-provoking interviews, Wehr seeks to understand how such transformative responses arise. As we face a world of deepening divides and the necessity for collaborative action,*

*this moving account has much to teach us about how we can rediscover and affirm our common humanity.*"
— Olivia Stokes Dreier, Senior Peacebuilding Advisor and Former Executive Director, Karuna Center for Peacebuilding

"*When archetypal evil takes on a human face, the challenge is no longer about defeating evil, but holding on to what makes us most human. In this eloquently and insightfully written book, Demaris Wehr, weaves a beautiful tapestry of stories that illustrate the profound difficulty and power of holding on to truth, love, and forgiveness in order to triumph over unimaginable cruelty and injustice. This book and its stories of heroic courage, resilience, and determination are more relevant for our world today than ever before.*"
— Loralee M. Scott, Founder and Director, The Sophia Center for Transformative Learning

"*The horrors of the Bosnian war have been well-documented, and yet if the world is not to see that region descend into war again, then Milka Marinković's observation is crucial: All three nations in Bosnia-Herzegovina—Bosnian Muslims (Bosniaks), Bosnian Serbs, and Bosnian Croats—need to reenvision history. Presently, each nation has a story justifying its actions and its position. We need one story. Relating experiences from all sides of the conflict, Demaris Wehr gives this community, and us, a common narrative. She offers us insight into forgiveness and reconciliation from the frontlines of anguish. The wisdom of the narrators in this volume is wisdom that seems particularly apt and necessary at this moment in history: Forgiveness is about leaving the negative energy behind and having space for positive energy. As Sabiha Husić reminds us, 'It's important to distinguish between forgiving and forgetting.'*"
— The Rev. Canon Mpho Tutu van Furth, Executive Director of the Tutu Teach Foundation and coauthor with Archbishop Desmond Tutu of *The Book of Forgiving and Made for Goodness*

© 2020 by Chiron Publications. All rights reserved. No part of this publication may be reproduced, stored in a retrieval system, or transmitted, in any form by any means, electronic, mechanical, photocopying, recording, or otherwise, without the prior written permission of the publisher, Chiron Publications, P.O. Box 19690, Asheville, N.C. 28815-1690.

www.ChironPublications.com

Interior design by Danijela Mijailovic
Cover design by Lisa Carta
Cover Photograph "View of Kovaci Cemetery in Sarajevo. Bosnia and Herzegovina" by Nikolai Korzhov | Dreamstime.com
Printed primarily in the United States of America.

ISBN  978-1-63051-846-2 paperback
ISBN  978-1-63051-847-9 hardcover
ISBN  978-1-63051-848-6 electronic
ISBN  978-1-63051-849-3 limited edition paperback


Library of Congress Cataloging-in-Publication Data Pending

# Dedication

I dedicate *Making It Through* to the eight Bosnian survivors
I was honored to interview for this book, to the thousands of
others who suffered during the war there, and to Paula Green,
whose outstanding work for peace and reconciliation in Bosnia
and around the world inspires me every day.

# Contents

Part III— Conclusion

# Foreword

We human beings live with unrelenting conflicts, within and between ourselves. We are hardwired to promote and protect ourselves when we feel threatened. As singer-songwriter Leonard Cohen wisely reminds us in his song "Different Sides," we often find ourselves in a conflict that we did not intend to create, facing an opposition that seems enraging. Even though we aspire to unity or oneness in our heart of hearts, we frequently feel we need to fight for what we believe in.

And so, the drive to create enemies—by blaming and shaming others—is universal in our families, communities, societies, and nations. To resist and overcome it requires great skill and insight. All the world's religions have in common the teachings of both restraint and new perspectives that can bring about forgiveness and repair. In *Making It Through*, Demaris Wehr presents powerful stories and accounts that bring clearly into view a path from war to wisdom.

As a therapist, I see how often we are at war with ourselves, with opposing desires and motivations that pull us in opposite directions. In the US, we wage wars against cancer, drugs, bullying, political rivals, and especially those whose worldview is different from ours. We feel overwhelmed by rage and what we perceive as danger from the "other." Wars—whether military, social, cultural, racial, religious, or inner—promote chaos and delusion. And when license to act out is encouraged, as it is today in so many parts of the world, we witness humanity at its worst.

Dr. Wehr shares the insights of eight men and women who lived through one of these hellish times, ethnic cleansing in the former Yugoslavia. Reading their reflections on that period, which she presents faithfully in their own words, we see how it is possible to survive, and to hope, trust, and even thrive after such devastating hostility. These narrators each had a *centerpost*, an essential trait or focus that supported them not to demonize the "other side," and through holding strong to this mast, they were able to experience transformation even amid and especially after the genocidal Bosnian war.

The violence, rape, and destruction of that war were especially egregious insofar as they were perpetrated for the most part by those who had previously been friends, neighbors, colleagues, and teachers, without proximate provocation. Sectarian tribalism emerged, and communities were ripped apart as though out of the blue. But this was not something appearing from nothing; the hatred and enmity had been simmering beneath the surface for half a millennium, since the conquest of the region by the Ottoman Empire. Dr. Wehr explains clearly this role of intergenerational trauma, and how potent and toxic it is, and how bringing what is simmering into consciousness is essential so we aren't blindsided by what is knowable but not known.

The Bosnian tragedy illustrates how easily we human beings can turn against each other when shadow projections and ancient wounds rip apart the fabric of our interdependence. Demaris Wehr went to Bosnia six times and checked back with her narrators repeatedly to "get it right," so they could tell their stories in their own words in ways they precisely endorsed. What we read here is, consequently, transformative, fresh, authentic, and eye-opening.

Polly Young-Eisendrath, PhD
Worcester, Vermont
February 2020

2

# Note to the Reader

Nothing in my own life resembles going through genocide. Though many trials, challenges, and setbacks have beset me, a violent war in my country is not one of them. Even though my country has been implicated in terrible wars in other countries and I have experienced, as most readers have, the lockdown associated with the global pandemic of 2020, the chaos of complete disruption and destruction of life all around me and betrayal by friends and neighbors has not been my experience. Thus, I cannot begin to comprehend the suffering of those who survived the ethnic cleansing in Bosnia. However, I can *listen* to them with all my heart, trying to understand and convey their stories faithfully.

Even though the particularities of our lives are so different, the universality in their accounts became clear to me as I was about halfway through writing. At the time, my husband was dying and my mind was becoming disoriented, and these narrators' stories were able to guide me in *making it through* that most difficult experience. Each of their paths helped keep me on solid ground.

These accounts are not meant to be depressing. They have their horror, but in the midst of the horror, life and love persisted. The narratives of these Bosnian survivors not only guided me in my own life but also reignited my lifelong hope for world peace and restored my confidence in the power of truth to help us usher it in. I hope that reading these stories of trauma, transcendence, and truth will offer you solace and hope, as well.

# Part I
# Introduction

*"Only Connect…."*
— E.M. Forster

Map of Bosnia and Herzogovina

Bosnia and Herzegovina, also called "Bosnia-Herzegovina" or simply Bosnia, is a country on the Balkan Peninsula in southeastern Europe. Sarajevo, its capital and largest city, is located on the Miljacka River, surrounded by the Dinaric Alps. Bosnia is bordered by Croatia to the north, west, and south; Serbia to the east; Montenegro to the southeast; and the Adriatic Sea to the south, with a coastline twelve miles long surrounding the city of Neum.

9

# Introduction

Imagine yourself, if you can, in a place you cherish. Perhaps it's a spot where you played as a child: your home, your grandmother's garden, maybe a cottage on the shore where your family summered, or the neighborhood market where you shopped with your aunt, or just anywhere that gives you peace. Imagine the sense of peace and well-being that permeated this place.

Now, imagine that same place overrun by unspeakable atrocities—the corner store where you bought cool drinks in summer being looted and shelled, the teachers who guided you through school furnishing guns to your neighbors-turned-enemies. Your most cherished place has suddenly become a nexus of chaos, uncertainty, and fear. This was the experience of all too many Bosnians in the early 1990s.

Until April 1992, Bosnian Muslims, Croats, Serbs, Jews, and those of mixed identities lived together in peace—drinking Turkish coffee in cafés in Baščaršija, Sarajevo's old quarter, eating buttery baklava, singing folk songs late into the night, intermarrying, and dwelling in what they thought was bucolic serenity. Then, with almost no warning, their lives were shattered by a crusade of terror against Bosniaks (Bosnian Muslims) that raged for three-and-a-half years. Croats, Romani, Jews, and some Serbs were also victimized, but Bosniaks were the primary targets. Three hundred-fifty thousand people were killed during a campaign of ethnic cleansing, mass murder, and rape. In the small town of Srebrenica, 8,000 unarmed Bosniaks, mostly men and boys, were massacred in what the International Court of Justice has called a genocide.

This book includes the stories of that sudden heart-wrenching madness: villages shelled, innocents shot down in the village square, doctors hoarding medicines, libraries burning, families crowded into basements, parents sneaking children through tunnels in the middle of the night, and displaced sons huddling together in refugee camps. Paradoxically, this is also the story of shining jewels, of the possibilities of hope in the midst of profound desolation. It was in the power of this paradox that this book was born.

My passion for peace was ignited at a training called The Forum, held in Boston in the late 1990s. After a group process that included days of soul-searching with rigorous help from The Forum's trainers, I realized my life's purpose and I declared it in front of a group of 500 people: *"I stand for the possibility of peace."* For the first time, I realized that this was what I had "stood for" all my life. The support of all those people and the training itself activated a desire that was already within me. Not long after, my friend Olivia Hoblitzelle invited my husband and me to a fundraising dinner at her house, where Dr. Paula Green, the director and founder of the Karuna Center for Peacebuilding, was showing slides of her work in Bosnia. I found one of Paula's slides particularly arresting. It showed Muslim and Serb women in a cold, dark basement hotel room in postwar Bosnia. The women wore fur coats and hats inside the building. The lines on their stark faces showed undeniable pain from the recent war. These women had invited Paula to Bosnia to help them dialogue about their postwar conflicts.

Right then it was clear I would go to Bosnia. Paula and I were seated across from one another at the table. Reaching over and touching her hand, I said, "Please take me with you to Bosnia." My uncharacteristic boldness was the result of the deep intention of standing for peace uncovered at The Forum training. This was the beginning of my experience of what it meant to stand for peace.

Paula suggested I attend a course she would be giving on peacebuilding at the School for International Training, in Brattleboro, Vermont, that summer, which I did as well as the next. After that, she invited me to become a Karuna Center associate, which meant I could join an ongoing project. I chose Bosnia.

The Karuna Center's project in Bosnia was called "Projekt Diacom," which meant "Dialogue Project." It lasted five years—a few weeks of short-term, intensive work in peacebuilding each summer with a group combining the two ethnicities most implicated in the recent war, Bosnian Serbs and Bosnian Muslims (Bosniaks), and assignments during the year. The twenty participants were all educators. Two Croat women, Lutvija Rostov and Vesna Arkova, served as translators for the complex, delicate process of building understanding and compassion between the two groups.[1]

I joined Projekt Diacom the summer of 2000. We met in the town of Neum, which is colorful and fresh, overflowing with flower and vegetable gardens, and defined by the sparkling Adriatic Sea that embraces it. Hostilities in Bosnia had ended less than five years earlier, and streaks of wry, even humorous graffiti were everywhere. Bullet holes still pocked storefronts and vacant buildings. We met at a beachfront hotel that had been built during the Stalin era, when socialist architecture was at its least aesthetic. The hotel's concrete walls were drab and solid.

In the hundred-degree (Fahrenheit) heat, the air hung heavy in our bedrooms. One large room in the basement was

---

[1] See Arie Farnam, "The Hard Work of Getting Along," *Christian Science Monitor,* August 14, 2001, about Projekt Diacom, https://www.csmonitor.com/2001/0814/p13s1-leca.html

air-conditioned, and so we met there for our trainings. These twenty high school principals, teachers, counselors, and other educators from the two main ethnicities that had been in lethal conflict only a few years earlier were now engaged in a fragile process of rebuilding understanding and compassion. Paula, a gifted trainer and facilitator, addressed these delicate dynamics with skill.

After the morning trainings, we would eat lunch and walk to the beach, arriving there through a tunnel beneath the hotel. My skin crawled as we made our way through that dark, damp passageway, which had been a hiding place for Bosniaks while Serb gunfire raged outside. The eerie sensation of evils committed there lingered, even after we left the tunnel and reentered the breezy sea air at the beach, where sparkling sunlight danced on the sea and children laughed and played. When we returned to the hotel through that dark space, and back into our air-conditioned room, participants continued to wrestle with their experiences of the recent war. Sometimes the struggle was so intense that I held my breath, riveted on the unfolding process, and wondering how Paula was going to handle it. Gradually, some of the participants learned to trust some members of the other group.

I was part of Projekt Diacom for three of its five years. After that, I returned to Bosnia three more times, first, to attend a small seminar in Sarajevo sponsored by the Karuna Center. We were a group of twelve Americans learning about the Bosnian war and its aftermath from a handpicked group of outstanding Bosnian survivors. I returned two more times, once to interview the eight narrators of this book and once more for follow-up interviews.

All the survivors I met in Bosnia had a compelling depth, but during the trainings, it never occurred to me to write a book about them. The idea of writing dawned on me gradually during the follow-up seminar sponsored by the Karuna Center. I can only describe this as an alchemical process whose beginnings were mysterious, like a seed planted in the dark soil. That seed had been planted during The Forum, where I'd stood for peace. Then the seed went underground, germinating. When conditions were right for the sprouting—temperature, soil, sunlight, rain—I found myself in propitious circumstances. Reconnecting with Vahidin Omanović from the Projekt Diacom trainings at the Sarajevo seminar, our friendship deepened. I was reminded of Milka Marinković and Senka Jakupović, two interviewees you will meet later in the book. Like Vahidin, they were Neum graduates, although they were not at the seminar. Vahidin's presence reminded me of them. And I reconnected with Marijana Senjak and Sabiha Husić, whom I'd met at the early trainings in Brattleboro. They were also at the Sarajevo seminar and took me under their wings. Linking arms as we walked together and bringing me tea when I was cold, I was deeply touched by their willingness to talk to me about difficult subjects.

Three seminar speakers, Jakob Finci, Salih Rasavać, and Vjekoslav Saje, inspired me by their truth-telling, their humor, and their lightness of spirit. Near the end of the seminar, I tentatively asked each of these eight survivors if they would agree to be interviewed, and to my great surprise, each of them responded with a resounding "yes."

The brutalities that took place in the Balkans in the early 1990s were beyond anything the world had seen since the Second World War. These atrocities included rape, mutilation, murder, torture, and more. They have been thoroughly reported on in other media. Though Part II of this book includes stories describing horrifying events that happened during the war, this book focuses on how the narrators "made it through." Each of these eight inter-viewees described holding onto what I now call a *centerpost*—forgiveness, humility, devotion to family, integrity, faith, optimism, duty, and transcendence—under the extremely challenging conditions of war.

These interviewees were not concentration camp survivors or victims of rape or physical torture, but each suffered mental torture as well as physical hardship being in a "field" in which atrocities impossible to predict or control were taking place. All eight narrators lost friends or family. Some were in refugee camps. Some went through the anguish of family members dying, only to find a member alive afterward, while others assumed family members were alive, only to find in the end that they had died. All had their sense of what was real and reliable turned upside down. They were able to stabilize themselves by relying on their "grit" as they made their way through horrors beyond words. They also counted on each other. Knowing that others were out there doing their best, helped them as well. Yet some nearly drowned emotionally with the horror of it all, if not during the war, then afterward when they could think about it.

Trying to put myself in their place and finding it impossible, hearing each new horror during their interviews, I asked, "How did you make it through *that*?" In the process, repeating the question and by listening to *this* event, *that* atrocity, *this* loss, *that* rescue, whatever came up in their stories, I would ask again, "How did you make it through *that?*" They told me, and in the process of this book's gestation, I gradually understood the profundity of their answers. They came back again and again to their core, sustaining principles, and I witnessed what the best of humanity can do under the worst of circumstances.

We still live in the worst of circumstances in many parts of the world, usually not of this magnitude, but atrocious, sobering situations that belong to all of us. Crises like those in Rwanda, Cambodia, and Bosnia, and today in Yemen and

Syria, remind us that normalcy can turn 180 degrees in a moment. Even a Nobel Peace Prize winner, Aung San Suu Kyi, has in recent years not stopped an ethnic cleansing in her country of Myanmar (Burma).[2]

Twenty-five years after the official ending of the Bosnian war and genocide, Bosnia is still very much in the news. In March 2016, Radovan Karadžić, one of the single most heinous manufacturers of this massacre, was indicted at The Hague for crimes against humanity and genocide in Srebrenica and sentenced to forty years in prison, a term well beyond his life span.[3] In May 2016, *PBS News Hour* featured a ten-minute segment on the current conditions in Bosnia-Herzegovina, which are still desperate. In the fall of 2017, the infamous "butcher of Bosnia," Ratko Mladić, was convicted of war crimes and genocide at The Hague.[4] Shortly afterward,

---

[2] Rights groups and UN leaders condemned the escalating violence and atrocities, which were described by a number of observers as ethnic cleansing and crimes against humanity. The clashes and exodus created what UN Secretary-General Antonio Guterres called a "humanitarian and human rights nightmare." At an emergency UN Security Council meeting, US Ambassador to the United Nations Nikki Haley said Myanmar authorities carried out "brutal, sustained campaign to cleanse the country of an ethnic minority," and she called on members to suspend weapons provisions to the military." Aung San Suu Kyi, Myanmar's de facto leader, has denied that ethnic cleansing is taking place and dismissed international criticism of her handling of the crisis, accusing critics of fueling resentment between Buddhists and Muslims in the country. In September 2017, the Nobel Peace Prize laureate said her government had "already started defending all the people in Rakhine in the best way possible." In December, the Myanmar government denied access to the UN Special Rapporteur on human rights in Myanmar, Yanghee Lee, and suspended cooperation for the remainder of her term. Eleanor Albert and Andrew Chatzky, "The Rohingya Crisis," Council on Foreign Relations Backgrounder, December 5, 2018, https://www.cfr.org/backgrounder/rohingya-crisis

[3] Radovan Karadžić, born June, 19, 1945, is a Bosnian Serb former politician and convicted war criminal who served as the President of Republika Srpska during the Bosnian War and sought the unification of that entity with Serbia.

[4] "The former Bosnian Serb commander Ratko Mladić, nicknamed the 'butcher of Bosnia,' was sentenced to life imprisonment after being convicted of

former Bosnian war criminal Slobodan Praljak, upon hearing his conviction in court, publicly drank poison and died soon after. And on July 8, 2018, *PBS News Hour* featured a ten-minute segment titled "Adults Born from Wartime Assault in Bosnia Search for Paths to Justice."[5]

As Vjekoslav Saje, one of the interviewees in this book, said to me, referring to the war in his country: "It was good and evil fighting. Not Serbs and Muslims fighting, but good and evil fighting."[6] I understood Vjeko to mean that the war in Bosnia was bigger than just people at war with one another; that it had a quality of genuine evil, an archetypal dimension that is impersonal, gripping, and deeply frightening. At that level, evil, like good, transcends the human condition and can engulf it. We must be prepared.

At the beginning of each interview, I present a quote that I believe is that survivor's most brilliant insight. Although

---

genocide, war crimes, and crimes against humanity. More than twenty years after the Srebrenica massacre, Mladic was found guilty at the United Nations-backed international criminal tribunal for the former Yugoslavia (ICTY) in The Hague of ten offences involving extermination, murder and persecution of civilian populations. As he entered the courtroom, Mladić gave a broad smile and thumbs up to the cameras—a gesture that infuriated victims' relatives. His defiance shifted into detachment as the judgment began: Mladić played with his fingers and nodded occasionally, looking initially relaxed. The verdict was disrupted for more than half an hour when he asked the judges for a bathroom break. After he returned, defense lawyers requested that proceedings be halted or shortened because of his high blood pressure. The judges denied the request. Mladić then stood up shouting, "This is all lies" and "I'll fuck your mother." He was forcibly removed from the courtroom. The verdicts were read in his absence." Owen Bowcott and Julian Borger, "Ratko Mladić convicted of war crimes and genocide at UN Tribunal, *Guardian*, November 22, 2017, https://www.theguardian.com/world/2017/nov/22/ratko-mladic-convicted-of-genocide-and-war-crimes-at-un-tribunal

[5] See https://thejptimes.wordpress.com/2018/07/08/adults-born-from-wartime-assault-in-bosnia-search-for-paths-to-justice/

[6] See Chapter 10, Vjekoslav's chapter, for his remarkable insights about the nature of evil.

each had many profound insights, the one I chose is, to me, a shining gem, a beautiful stone placed on a path made up of stones that lead to a conclusion about how one can make it through a crisis as huge as genocide. Following that is a quote by another thinker, author, or poet. It is an accompaniment, like a piano accompanying a soloist; a companion from another culture who has found something of a similar nature he or she has expressed in writing.

The quotes from the interviewees illustrate how the alchemical process described by Jung as "individuation" can wrestle gold from the worst of human circumstances. The quotes by others—silent witnesses—show that we are all in this search for peace, clarity, purpose, resilience, and wholeness together. After a brief introduction, each of the interview chapters shares the interviewee's own words, abridged for this book.

After the "ethnic cleansing" of the 1990s, you may have thought of the Balkans as a place of bestiality. After reading this book, I hope you will also see it as a place of love and light and come to think of these Bosnians as our neighbors, teachers, and friends. The lessons their stories offer range from forgiveness under impossible circumstances to humility, love of family, integrity, faith, duty, optimism, and transcendence, showcased even more brilliantly because they arose during a time where the best and worst sides of humanity were fully on display.

Part II presents the stories and centerposts of each of these eight inspiring individuals. These narrators share their pieces of a greater mosaic, and through them all, we experience the hope, courage, and humanity that were needed for them to make it through and are needed for us to make it through the challenging times that face us now.

As the opening quote from E.M. Forster tells us, "Only connect." When all is said and done, this book is about truthful connection and the arduous process of finding and holding onto it in the midst of a world once again gone awry.

# Chapter 1
# The Centerpost

*"If you don't trust yourself, if you don't know
your own value system, then you're lost,
and you can be manipulated."*
— Salih Rasavać, Social Worker, Sarajevo

Walking through the woods in West Tisbury, Massachusetts, one fall afternoon, musing about the interviews, it occurred to me that all the narrators had an outstanding character strength that sustained them during their trials. It was almost as if each one had a hidden rudder guiding them through the storm. What could I call this ineffable quality, this *essence* or instinct that enabled them to act in such admirable ways? An image flashed into my mind of Odysseus lashed to a mast in the middle of his ocean sail to avoid the deadly temptation of the Sirens. Then a word, "centerpost," flashed in my mind as well. Odysseus had found something that would enable him to arrive home safely to his wife, Penelope, and his son, Telemachos. He clung to a literal mast—a "centerpost"—that would both strengthen and restrain him through a challenge so difficult that, without that much resolve, he would not have made it.

Likewise, the Bosnians needed an internal mast, a centerpost, to keep them from flailing about and drowning, losing their centers and their souls. Consider Salih Rasavać, a graceful, middle aged, nonpracticing Muslim. He is a former folk dancer and a social worker, graced with a tall slender frame, big brown eyes, a radiant smile, and expressive gestures. In the course of my interview with him, Salih literally told me what his centerpost is: optimism. His ability to be optimistic sustained him as he acted altruistically throughout the war on behalf of others. It still characterizes him now. Next, Marijana Senjak came to mind. Marijana, a Croat psychologist, spoke frequently of the ever-present necessity of making agonizing choices during the war. She did this through holding to her centerpost of inviolable integrity. Senka Jakupović, a mother, wife, and later a fitness trainer and peacebuilder, has as her centerpost devotion to family. She made it through by focusing on her husband and children, and finally finding the truth of her husband's whereabouts. Jakob Finci, a prominent leader of Sarajevo's Jewish community, also told me directly what his centerpost was: duty. Each interviewee revealed a central quality, an innate part of their character, that guided them through the crisis and enabled them to help others as well, while providing an example of behaving with integrity.

Although visually the term may conjure up something rigid, the word is used here to describe something fluid, dynamic, and upright, that grounds one in the middle of insanity. It may not be a consciously held value, but an instinctive one until it is brought forth in a dire situation. In the course of each interview, these central governing values surfaced, but only years later, when we discussed them, did they become conscious of them. Our central values can help us make it through seemingly impossible challenges.

All eight narrators in this book made it through by helping others during the crisis and by staying connected to their own souls in this time of profound disconnection from both. They didn't wait until they were healed to help. They were reeling, staggering, and stunned, and they didn't have time to process the trauma while it was happening. Had they been *feeling* the overwhelming emotions at the time the crisis was happening to them, it might have paralyzed them. They were confused at the time, and they did what they could to cope. Later, after the immediate crisis had passed, they felt the feelings and suffered them consciously. This nonfeeling, proactive, life-affirming response during a crisis is a self-protective mechanism, and it helped them survive with less damage.

Resisting extreme inner impulses in desperate situations is difficult and requires unusual self-discipline. It is hard not to be overtaken internally (psychologically, mentally, spiritually) in situations of global chaos and confusion. Like Odysseus, these Bosnians lashed themselves to a mast when they were presented with unimaginably difficult circumstances. This metaphorical mast prevented them from following the crowd and joining in the mass hysteria.

Holding to a centerpost has the ability to ripple outward and affect the whole. As noted Swiss psychiatrist C.G. Jung wrote in 1936, before World War II broke out: "The man of the past is alive in us today to a degree undreamt of before the war, and *in the last analysis what is the fate of great nations but a summation of the psychic changes in individuals?*"[7]

Warning us of the possibility of mass possession, Jung also wrote: "Since neuroses are in most cases not just private concerns, but social phenomena, we must assume that archetypes are constellated in these cases too.... *There is no lunacy people under the domination of an archetype will not fall a prey to.*"[8]

---

[7] C.G. Jung, *Collected Works, Volume 9,1. The Archetypes and the Collective Unconscious.* Bollingen Series XX. (New York: Princeton University Press, 1969). 47.

[8] Jung, *The Archetypes and the Collective Unconscious.* 47-48. For the reader unfamiliar with the term "archetype", see Wehr, *Jung and Feminism*, pp. 51-52. An archetype, in the popular use of the term, is an image, a primordial image, or energy-field, found in all cultures everywhere, although in different forms. An archetypal image therefore carries universal, instinctual power. People can become "possessed" by archetypal energy, by the strong emotional content of the images, by ancient grievances, hatred, etc., especially when the people are

Clinging to our central values helps us live for others and not fall prey to the distorted reality that surrounds us, a field so frightening that many people act out of desperation, caught by the archetype of which Jung speaks. Being "possessed" or dominated by the archetype of war and losing all sense of reason, love, and connection, is the lunacy the narrators of these stories did not fall prey to.

Centerposts sustain us through terrible actions by others. They help us focus on the good and not get drawn into the evil surrounding us. This does not mean we should ignore the evil. Clinging to the good, the centerpost, guides us out of numbness and into caring and altruism, into the best versions of ourselves, under the worst of circumstances.

Centerposts are not always individual. Collectively held values also provide strength in a time of crisis. Sarajavo's daily newspaper, *Oslobodjenje,* whose name means "liberation" in Bosnian, was established in 1943 as a protest against Nazism. The *Oslobodjene* staff kept the newspaper running through conditions of unbelievable hardship during the entire war in Bosnia. From the Serbs' opening fire on civilians in Sarajevo in April 1992 to the end of the war in November 1995, *Oslobodjenje* was available on the newsstands every day except one. When the electricity was off because of nearly constant power outages, the newspaper staff produced *Oslobodjenje* anyway. Even when militant Serbs bombed the ten-story building that housed the

in a "force-field" dominated by one or more of these archetypal images. It takes great self-awareness and self-control to avoid falling into this energy field, prey to these powerful unconscious forces. Jung distinguishes in his later works between this energy field and its images, and the archetype *per se.* Due to the brevity of this discussion, I will retain the popular use of the term *archetype* here, referring to the image, the energy, and the force-field.

newspaper, the staff still brought the paper out every morning by carrying the ancient news-printing equipment into a bomb shelter beneath the building and working all night by candlelight and kerosene lamps, churning out the newspaper by hand.

In speech at a seminar in Sarajevo sponsored by the Karuna Center, Senka Kurtavić, then editor of the newspaper, explained, "In a situation of such horrible abnormality, it was important to maintain normalcy. People like to go to a cafe, drink their morning coffee, and read their morning paper. We provided them with that. *Oslobodenje* went from being a daily newspaper to a mission." The work of the newspaper galvanized the staff and gave them a singular focus and sense of purpose.[9]

By doing what is truly in our neighbor's best interest, we serve our own best interest and give ourselves a purpose for living. In a time when it would be easy to descend into despair, maintaining normalcy can, in itself, be a core collective value, one that the staff of *Oslobodenje* clung to without fail.

By holding to a centerpost, each of the Bosnian narrators found a grounding point to keep going. Most of them sprang into action during the war, as did the journalists producing *Oslobodenje*. Action, rather than passivity, has been shown to help trauma survivors be less damaged. As Dan Goleman points out in *Emotional Intelligence*, "The operative word is *uncontrollable*. If people feel there is something they can do in a catastrophic situation, some control they can exert, no matter how minor, they fare far better emotionally than those

---

[9] In 1993, *Oslobodenje* was awarded the Sakharov Prize for Freedom of Thought. The editors of *Oslobodenje*, Kemal Kurspahić and Gordana Knezević, were named International Editors of the Year for 1993 by the World Press Review for their "bravery, tenacity, and dedication to the principles of journalism." During the war, its staff consisted of Bosniaks, Bosnian Serbs, and Bosnian Croats.

who feel utterly helpless. The element of helplessness is what makes a given event *subjectively* overwhelming."[10]

Bringing forth their centerpost values sustained and connected these Bosniaks, Croats, and Serbs through near-starvation, sniper fire, refugee camps, and the loss of home and family. Years after the war and the genocide, the eight narrators of this book have healed enough to help themselves and others deal with the effects of the brutalities they all endured. Each of the narrators presented in *Making It Through* has a strong desire to end war worldwide, and most believe it's possible. In the postwar years, despite ongoing political, economic, and social upheaval in Bosnia, these individuals continue to promote actions that contribute to the greater good.

---

[10] Daniel Goleman, *Emotional Intelligence: Why It Can Matter More Than IQ* (New York, Bantam Books, 1995), 204.

## Chapter 2
# How Beautiful Bosnia Became
# Host to Concentration Camps

*"How is it possible that this culture-loving era*
*could be so monstrously callous and amoral? How is it*
*conceivable that all our lauded technological progress—our*
*very civilization—should become like an axe,*
*in the hands of the pathological criminal?"*
— Albert Einstein

The Turkish Ottoman Empire invaded the Kingdom of
Bosnia in the fifteenth century and annexed it into its
Empire.[11] Bosnia remained under Ottoman rule for 400 years.
During that time, the Ottomans brought Islam to the region.
In accord with the Muslim system of "protected persons,"
Christians and Jews who already resided in Bosnia when it
became part of the Ottoman Empire were guaranteed the right
to worship. Over the years, many Turkish Muslims, Bosnian
Serbs, and Bosnian Croats intermarried.

In the nineteenth century, Bosnia became part of the
Austro-Hungarian Monarchy, which lasted until World War I.

---

[11] The Balkan region that is now Bosnia-Herzogovina has had permanent
settlements since the Neolithic Era. By the early historical period, it was peopled
by Illyrians and Celts. Christianity arrived in the first century, and by the fourth
century, the area had become part of the Western Roman Empire. Germanic
tribes invaded, followed by Slavs in the sixth century. In 1136, Hungary invaded
Bosnia but allowed it to be essentially autonomous. In 1377, Bosnia was
proclaimed a kingdom.

In the period between World Wars I and II, Bosnia was part of the Kingdom of Yugoslavia. After the Allied victory in World War II, Yugoslavia (formally "the Socialist Federal Republic of Yugoslavia") was established as a country with six republics: Bosnia, Croatia, Macedonia, Montenegro, Serbia, and Slovenia. In addition, two autonomous provinces were set up within Serbia: Vojvodina and Kosovo. The war in Bosnia that took place between 1992 and 1995 arose directly from this history, not because of "ancient ethnic hatreds," as the West was led to believe, but because of the unaddressed, unhealed, centuries-long buildup of Serb resentment at having been conquered. This is discussed further in "How Did This Happen?" (See p. 36)

Part of the 1992-95 war in Bosnia was officially declared a genocide by the International Court of Justice in The Hague.[12] Literally *genocide* means the intentional killing of a race of people. The definition of genocide in Barbara Colorusso's book, *Extraordinary Evil: A Short Walk to Genocide,* is "the planned, deliberate destruction of a people."[13] Genocide has been referred to as "the crime without a name," meaning that it's almost beyond our ability to imagine or believe it.

At the time of their interviews, these Bosnians had endured a war that escalated officially to genocide in Srebrenica, where nearly 8,000 unarmed Bosniak men and boys were murdered. The death toll taken by the war in the whole

---

[12] February 26, 2007, was the first time in history that the International Court of Justice called the 1995 massacre of Bosnian Muslims at Srebrenica an act of genocide but "determined that Serbia itself was not guilty of the enormous crime. ... The ruling resulted from a civil lawsuit Bosnia had brought against Serbia, the first in which one country sued another for genocide." Marlise Simons. "Court Declares Bosnia Killings Were Genocide," *New York Times,* February 27, 2007, https://www.nytimes.com/2007/02/27/world/europe/27hague.html

[13] Barbara Coloroso, *Extraordinary Evil: A Short Walk to Genocide* (New York: Nation Books, 2007), 1.

of Bosnia was estimated in 1994 at around 200,000 by Cherif Bassouni, head of the UN expert commission investigating war crimes.[14,15] By the fall of 1993 in Sarajevo alone, "10,000 Sarajevans were dead and 56,000 wounded, of whom 15,000 were children. The total mortality figure in Sarajevo would rise to 12,000."[16]

From April 1992 until December 1995, the Serbs officially perpetrated war and genocide against their friends and neighbors, the Bosniaks (Muslims), who were officially the victims. The Croats switched sides midstream. At first, Croats were allied with the Bosniaks, confronting the Serbs. Later, they switched to an earlier alliance they had with Serbs. During that time, some Croats, joining Serbs, also perpetrated atrocities on their Bosniak neighbors. Finally, Croats switched back to their alliance with the Bosniaks. Croats and Bosniaks now share 51 percent of the country of Bosnia-Herzegovina, and Serbs control 49 percent.

The three main groups living in Bosnia-Herzegovina were, and are, Serbs (Eastern Orthodox Christian), Croats (Roman Catholics), and Bosniaks (Bosnian Muslims). When the war began, very few of them were practicing their religion. Many were intermarried and could not be classified as belonging to one group. They had enjoyed nearly forty years of peace and did not think much about these classifications. Yet, all of these intermingled ethnic groups, as well as other

---

[14] "Casualties in Bosnian War," 102.000 drept I Bosnia, NRK News, November 14, 2004, in Norwegian.

[15] Calculating the number of deaths that resulted from the conflict has been highly politicized. There are large discrepancies between estimates of the total number of casualties, ranging from 25,000 to 329,000. These are in part the result of the use of inconsistent definitions of "war victims." Some researchers calculated only direct casualties of military activity while others also included indirect casualties, such as those who died from harsh living conditions, hunger, cold, illnesses or other accidents indirectly caused by the war conditions.

[16] Elizabeth Pond. *Endgame in the Balkans: Regime Change, European Style* (Washington, DC: Brookings Institution, 2006). 27.

ethnicities, were involved in the war, and all of Bosnia's citizens endured terror and a living nightmare.

The media contributed to the West's misunderstanding of the war in Bosnia, seeing it as the resurgence of "ancient ethnic hatreds" and thus a civil war, but that explanation was deceptive. Slavic tribes had been intermingling with Turkish Muslims since the Ottoman Empire (Turks) conquered the area. Misha Glenny reminds us, Yugoslavs "were of the same ethnos." In *The Fall of Yugoslavia,* he writes:

"They are not ethnic conflicts, as the media would have it, as most of those doing the killing are of the same ethnos. Indeed, what is striking about Bosnia-Herzegovina in particular is just how closely related are the Serbs, the Croats, and the Muslims. Yet a broad perception has developed, outside the Balkans, that these are wars fueled by 'ancient hatreds,' as the British Prime Minister, John Major, has characterized them."[17]

The myth that these wars were fueled by ancient hatreds is what kept the war going so long. There was some truth to its being a civil war, but it was mostly ancient animosity, and this designation hid the fact of genocidal intent.

### What Happened?

Before wars for independence in Croatia, Slovenia, and Bosnia broke out in the early 1990s, the former Yugoslavia was the most prosperous and free socialist country in the Communist bloc. Yugoslavs were proud of their country, traveled freely to the West, where they purchased goods, and enjoyed their relative freedom. They had a rich cultural heritage and were well acquainted with Western literature,

---

[17] Misha Glenny. *The Fall of Yugoslavia.* (London: Penguin Books, 1992), 172, 183.

music, and art. From 1953 until 1980, Yugoslavia was led by Marshall Josip Broz Tito, a World War II hero and a Croat-Slovene, whose goal was unifying Yugoslavia. Tito's slogan, "Brotherhood and Unity," was the glue that kept the country together. Under his presidency, Croats, Bosniaks, Serbs, Jews, and those of mixed heritage lived together in apparent harmony. The interviewees in this book and other Bosnian friends spoke of this period with genuine longing.

After Tito's death in 1980, the country began to crumble. Tito had not prepared the country for a successor, and nationalism, which was breaking loose throughout Eastern Europe in the late 1980s and early '90s, also affected Yugoslavia. The republics that comprised the country began longing for their freedom. With Slobodan Milošević's election as president of the former Yugoslavia in 1989, the unraveling of its union began.

Eight entities (six republics and two autonomous provinces)[18] made up the whole of Yugoslavia when it began breaking into small, nationalistic states. In 1991, foreseeing the coming domination by Milošević, Slovenia and Croatia seceded from Yugoslavia. After brief wars with each, Milošević withdrew his forces, and the international community recognized them as sovereign. In contrast, when Bosnia declared independence and seceded from the former Yugoslavia in the spring of 1992, Milošević did not withdraw his army. Though the US and European nations recognized Bosnia's independence, as they had done with Slovenia and Croatia, Milošević refused. Instead, he attacked Sarajevo with its beautiful mosques, churches, and synagogues and its peaceful citizens of all the groups.

Bosnians of all ethnicities held nonviolent demonstrations in Sarajevo, their capital city, in early April of 1992

---

[18] The six republics are Croatia, Slovenia, Bosnia, Serbia, Macedonia, and Montenegro. The two provinces are Kosovo and Vojvodina.

to protest Milošević's refusal to honor their bid for independence. Serb snipers[19] responded by firing on them from high buildings and from hills surrounding the capital. This was the beginning of the war in Bosnia.

When sniper shots rang out from the garish, mustard-colored Holiday Inn, scattering civilians in the streets of Sarajevo on April 2, 1992, Westerners recognized the building from iconic photos they had seen of it in 1984 during the Winter Olympics. Whereas Sarajevo had previously been known for hosting the Olympics, it soon became known as the city where Serb snipers continued to shoot helpless civilians, eventually wounding over 15,000 children.[20]

During the siege, the citizens of Sarajevo risked sniper fire every day merely to cross a street. Milošević's army held them hostage and in terror, blocking all connection to the outside world and cutting off all supplies. As Elizabeth Pond writes in *Endgame in the Balkans:* "In many cases snipers, with a clear view from high rise buildings and the surrounding hillsides, have targeted the most vulnerable of civilians, including: children (even infants); persons carrying heavy plastic containers filled with water; persons in queues; pedestrians at intersections; and rescuers attempting to come to the aid of sniping and shelling victims."[21]

Beautiful Bosnia became host to concentration camps, torture, mass murder, rapes, and ethnic cleansing.[22] As the war

---

[19] *Serbs* here means Bosnian Serbs and Serbs from Serbia. Note that some Serbs stood with their compatriots wanting their independence from Yugoslavia.

[20] Pond, 26.

[21] Pond, 27.

[22] *Ethnic cleansing* is a euphemism for one ethnicity trying to wipe out another ethnicity. The term specifically refers to one group of people (in this case, the Serbs) forcing another group of people at gunpoint (in this case mostly Bosniaks, but some Croats) to leave their homes and go to another town. Often, the victims fled to towns the UN had declared "Safe Havens." Rather than finding safety in these towns, the "ethnically cleansed" Bosniaks were subjected to the horrors of a concentration camp, where they were tortured, maimed, and killed.

went on, Bosniaks and other Sarajevo citizens burned their books, shoes, and furniture to heat their stoves. People risked their lives to find water and bread, including highly educated, culturally elite citizens. Some, like our narrators Salih Rasavać and Vjekoslav Saje, sneaked their children out of Bosnia. Ironically, sending children abroad in this manner contributed to the fragmentation of Bosnian families. Intact families in Bosnia had been the norm before that and greatly cherished.[23]

Perhaps the worst cultural injustice occurred when the Serbs set fire to the world-famous National Library in Sarajevo. With the burning of this national treasure of modern Islam came the loss of millions of scientific, technological, Islamic, and other volumes of inestimable value. The burning of the National Library was an attack on the refinement, elegance, science, and religion of Sarajevans themselves. This wanton act was a horrifying symbol, a destruction of culture. Kemal Bakaršić, an eyewitness of this brutal act, writes: "The attack lasted less than half an hour. The fire lasted into the next day. The sun was obscured by the smoke of books, and all over the city sheets of burned paper, fragile pages of grey ashes, floated down like a dirty black snow. Catching a page you could feel its heat, and for a moment read a fragment of text in a strange kind of black and grey negative, until as the heat dissipated, the page melted to dust in your hand."[24]

---

[23] Many other factors contributed to this fragmentation. These include the death of male family members as they became soldiers, or as they were kidnapped, tortured, and killed. Other Bosnians made it to safe shores, such as the US, but they lost touch with their families that way. Many Bosniak women were raped and dishonored, forced to bear the children of the Serb perpetrators. Displacement from one section of Bosnia to the other was another contributing factor. Of course, some families did retain their former closeness in spite of all these obstacles.

[24] "On August 27, 1992, in the early morning, the National Library was deliberately attacked and burned. Twenty-five mortar shells struck the building, launched from four positions in the surrounding hills. In support of the attack,

Though the United Nations sent peacekeepers to the Balkans in 1992, declaring six towns "safe havens," and although these UN peacekeepers patrolled the streets, the peacekeepers' hands were tied by orders not to shoot unless their own lives were directly threatened. Thus, they stood by helplessly during the murderous mayhem in Sarajevo and other parts of Bosnia. The UN's "safe havens" were completely unsafe. Serbs not only attacked the towns; they also attacked the UN peacekeepers.

Residents were dismayed by the UN peacekeepers' impotence to intervene and equally confused by the US's policy of nonintervention. Throughout 1993, confident that the UN, the United States, and the European Community would not take military action, Serbs freely committed genocide against Muslims in Bosnia.[25] The death toll taken by the war in the whole of Bosnia was originally estimated in 1994 at around 200,000 by Cherif Bassouni, head of the UN expert commission investigating war crimes.[26]

On August 28, 1995, after the Serbs had laid siege to Sarajevo for nearly three years, a Bosnian Serb named Romanija Corps lobbed five mortar shells into "Markala," a colorful marketplace in the center of Sarajevo, where babushka-clad Bosnian women sold fresh vegetables, fruits, and other products. The young Serb killed thirty-seven innocent

---

forty shells were dropped on adjacent streets, preventing the fire brigade from coming into action. The odd thing about this supplementary attack is that the aggressors had cut off the water to the district before the attack, so there was no need to bomb the fire brigade. But they did it anyway." Kemal Bakaršić. *Life During Wartime: The Libraries of Sarajevo and the Book That Saved Our Lives.* Autumn 1994. www.newcombat.net/article thelibraries.html.

[25] United Human Rights Council. See, e.g. https://www.un.org/documents /ga/res/50/ares50-193.htm

[26] "Casualties in Bosnian War"; 102.000 drept I Bosnia, NRK News, November 14, 2004, in Norwegian.

shoppers and sellers and wounded ninety.[27] This act finally galvanized the Clinton administration.

The US and NATO intervened on August 30, 1995, when it brokered the first peace initiatives. Clinton issued an ultimatum through the North Atlantic Treaty Organization, demanding that the Serbs withdraw all their troops from Sarajevo. The Serbs complied, and a NATO-imposed cease-fire was declared. Although the Serbs officially "obeyed" the cease-fire, Serb snipers continued to attack Muslim towns in the six "safe havens," of which Sarajevo was one. The Dayton Accords, the international agreements that officially ended the war, were finalized and signed in November (in Paris) and December (in Dayton, Ohio), 1995.[28] Serbs went on destroying lives and property during the months between August and December. Though the signing of the Dayton Accords officially ended the war, the "solution" froze in place the displacements that had been created by ethnic cleansing. The accords gave the Serbs 49 percent of Bosnia and renamed it Republika Srpska. They gave the Bosniaks and Croats 51 percent of Bosnia and called it The Federation. The whole country is called Bosnia-Herzegovina, which was its original name, shortened to Bosnia after the Austro-Hungarian war.

These postwar divisions have furthered nationalistic identities and fostered continued resentment as well as a

---

[27] Pond, 31.

[28] Richard Holbrooke, chief US peace negotiator, and Secretary of State Warren Christopher led the process by which the Dayton Peace Agreements were reached. The presidents of Bosnia, Croatia, and Serbia signed them on November 21, 1995, ending the war in Bosnia and outlining a General Framework Agreement for Peace in Bosnia and Herzegovina. The accords preserved Bosnia as a single state made up of two parts, the Bosniak-Croat federation and the Bosnian Serb Republic, with Sarajevo remaining as the undivided capital city. The agreement is known as the Dayton Accords, because the negotiations took place at the Wright-Patterson Air Force Base outside of Dayton, Ohio. They were signed again in Paris in December 1995, when the war officially ended.

longing for their prewar homes. The Dayton Accords ended the war and, at the same time, perpetuated the conditions for it, provoking even more resentment and permanent displacement.

## How Did This Happen?

*"Yugoslavia did not die a natural death; it was murdered, and Milošević, more than any other single leader, is responsible."*[29]
— Louis Sell, Milošević's biographer.

Although Slobodan Milošević, who became known as the "butcher of Serbia," was by no means solely responsible for this war, if there were only one person to hold accountable, it would be he. Milošević became president of the former Yugoslavia in 1989 (later of Serbia) and was the architect of this war, aided in crime by Franjo Tudjman, president of Croatia; Radovan Karadžić, a Bosnian Serb commander; and Ratko Mladić, also a Bosnian Serb commander. Milošević was charged with genocide at The Hague but died before his trial was finished.[30] Karadžić and Mladić were later convicted of genocide. Tudjman[31] was charged, although later exonerated.

---

[29] Pond, 9.

[30] The war crimes trial of Slobodan Milošević, the former President of Yugoslavia, at the International Criminal Tribunal for the former Yugoslavia (ICTY) lasted from February 2002 until his death in March 2006. Milošević faced 66 counts of crimes against humanity, genocide, and war crimes committed during the Yugoslav Wars of the 1990s. He pleaded not guilty to all the charges.

[31] Ian Traynor, "The Tudjman regime had been incriminated. Now it is exonerated. The result is joy in Zagreb and rancour in Belgrade. There was also bitterness from the dissenting two judges in the panel of five." *The Guardian.* November 16, 2012.

Milošević was born in 1941 in the small town of Pozarevać, fifty-five miles southeast of Belgrade, now in Serbia, and grew up during the 1940s and '50s, during the Axis invasion of Yugoslavia. His father, a Serbian Orthodox cleric, abandoned the family and committed suicide when Milošević was a young man. Slobodan's mother and uncle also committed suicide years later. He became a fervent member of the Communist youth party, rose up through the ranks, and was poised to take Tito's place some ten years after Tito's death.

While Tito used unification as a guiding philosophy, Milošević chose division. Vietnam War veteran Claude Anshin Thomas explains his perspective on this: "Without *specific awareness* of the intimate nature of our suffering, whatever that suffering may be, healing and transformation simply are not possible and we will continue to re-create that suffering and infect others with it."[32]

Repressed and unworked-through horrors inevitably erupt in later acts of violence within or without. Perhaps Milošević was driven by vengeance for his traumatic youth and inherited sense of victimization as a Serb. Like so many severely narcissistically wounded sociopaths, Milošević was duplicitous and charming. He manipulated with symbolic words and gestures, reawakening latent fears and unhealed ghosts of the past. Milošević's oratory charmed, excited, and magnetized, drawing huge crowds while revving up buried racism, ethnocentrism, and xenophobia. He refueled the Serbs' ancient fears of a Muslim takeover of their country, preparing the way for the destruction that would follow, including ethnically cleansing Bosniaks and creating a racially pure Greater Serbia. Not only were the Serb militants

---

[32] Claude Anshin Thomas: *At Hell's Gate: A Soldier's Journey from War to Peace.* (Boulder, Colorado: Shambhala Publications, 2006), 43

expected to follow this destructive trajectory, but for a period, the Croats joined them.[33]

Milošević whipped up the fear of a *jihad* in the Serbs by their Bosniak friends, neighbors and even family members. This was not grounded in the facts. Radical or fundamentalist Islam did not exist in Bosnia at the time. The prewar Muslims of Bosnia were gentle and peace-loving. Many of them did not practice religion, since religion was banned in Communism. Most urban, educated Bosniak women were not veiled. Bosnian Muslims had, and still have, a gentle, radiant, almost innocent sweetness about them. Urban dwelling Bosniaks were highly cultured, highly educated people, mainly secular. There was nothing threatening about them.

This sweetness is best exemplified by the Bosnian Muslims' central philosophy before the war, called "Merhamet," a practical and gracious kindness toward others and charity toward strangers.[34] Although most of the Bosnian Muslims did not actively practice their religion, they did practice Merhamet. This unspoken philosophy was, and still is, evident in the unusually gracious ways Bosniaks deal with conflicts, frustrations, and disappointments and in their hospitality.[35] Toward other people, they tended to see the good rather than focus on potential evil. Many Bosniaks today wonder if that attitude was naïve and if Merhamet should persist, especially if it makes them unprepared for the ills of this very flawed world.

Bosnian citizens of all ethnicities, as well as many Serb soldiers, were confused about what was going on. Some soldiers thought they were fighting a defensive war for a patriotic cause. Most were caught up in the madness, energy,

---

[33] See Resources (Appendix) for further reading.
[34] Conversation with Vahidin Omanović.
[35] For an in depth understanding of Merhamet, see Steven M. Weine, *When History is a Nightmare: Lives and Memories of Ethnic Cleansing in Bosnia-Herzegovina.* (New Brunswick, NJ: Rutgers University Press) 1999.

and panic-driven behavior of war. The collective energy and mass-mindedness, especially the madness of seeking revenge for hurts of earlier centuries, allowed them to become perpetrators of unspeakable atrocities.

### The Intergenerational Transmission of Trauma

Claude Anshin Thomas emphasizes the long-lasting effects of hidden wounds. If these wounds are not healed, passing them on is known as "the intergenerational transmission of trauma." Thomas tells the story of a young soldier from the Balkans who was shot in the arm by a sniper from his own group. Doctors from the other side saved him. The injured soldier was still stuck in blaming the other side, the "enemy" side. Thomas finally got him to recognize that the people on the "other side" were not all the same. After all, doctors from the *other side* had saved him. Finally, the soldier, softened, confided to Thomas: "This is not our war. It is our grandfathers' war. They should take up arms and fight. This is the politicians' war. They should be on the front lines."[36]

Vjekoslav Saje watched a young Serb musician on television, saying, "We are going to Istanbul. We were conquered by Turks there 500 years ago. We hope now we will win." Vjekoslav explained to me, "Somehow this young guy is still thinking about history, how his ancestors suffered and were conquered, and how he needs to take revenge."

This unconsciously held and intergenerationally transmitted attitude encourages humanity's lowest impulses to run rampant. When suffering is not made conscious and literally *suffered*, felt, and worked through, intergenerational trauma will prevail. Without conscious work on old and

---

[36] Thomas, *Hell's Gate*, 82-83.

ancestral wounds, people go numb and repeat old injuries, inflicting them on others for centuries to come.

By dredging up the old sense of persecution lurking in the Serb unconscious, Milošević created a driving force for his war on the Bosniaks. By the end of the war, nearly a quarter of a million people had been murdered. Perhaps even worse was the unquantifiable terror that remained: the loss of safety, dignity, faith, and belonging that those who survived are still enduring and having to repair.[37]

[37] Many thanks to Vjekoslav Saje who read and approved this chapter.

# Part II
# The Interviews

## The Karuna Center Participants
# Vahidin Omanović, Senka Jakupović, and Milka Marinković

When I first met Vahidin Omanović, Senka Jakupović, and Milka Marinković—three participants at Karuna Center for Peacebuilding's Projekt Diacom and the first interviewees in the book—they were not exemplifying their centerposts. They were still experiencing hell. They cried, they were angry and confrontational, and they struggled. At the same time, they had an undefined innate strength and beauty in them. They all lived near Neum, the seacoast location where we held these summer trainings. The beauty of Neum and the power of the trainings contributed greatly to their recovery.

43

*"There is no future without forgiveness."*
— Archbishop Desmond Tutu

# Chapter 3
# Vahidin Omanović
# Forgiveness

*"I'd rather be a victim than a victimizer."*

When I first met Vahidin Omanović (Vah-hée-dun O-máhn-o-vitch) at the Karuna Center training in the basement of the Moscow-style hotel in Neum, he was twenty-four years old, very traumatized, and very promising. He stood out for his courage, depth, and openness. In the summer of 2000, he was completing a Master's degree in Conflict Transformation in Brattleboro, Vermont, and continuing his summer program in Neum, Bosnia, his third time as a participant there. With his hearty welcome and radiant smile, Vahidin stole everyone's heart.

Nearly four years later, in May 2004, Vahidin had become an imam, Muslim priest, and was starting a dialogue project in his small village for Serbs and Bosniaks. His narrative affords a glimpse into the damage done to a young man's soul during the war and the ways he put himself back together again. Through his agonizing and healing journey with some special Serbs, Vahidin came to understand the shame that perpetrators carry and how damaging that can be. He ended up with the astonishing insight that he'd rather be a victim than a victimizer.

*Here is Vahidin Omanović in his own words:*
I grew up in the small village of Hrustava. In 1989, when I was fourteen, I went off to the Islamic Theological High School in Sarajevo. I never dreamed that one day I'd be forced to leave the place I was born and not be able to live with my parents, my sisters, and my brother.

I was sixteen, in my third year of high school, when the war began. I went home to our village for Ramadan. Normally, we'd stay in Sarajevo to help serve the community during Ramadan, but that year the Yugoslav Army (JNA) had moved into Bosnia, so we were sent home. In the town of Sanski Most, six miles from our village, Yugoslav soldiers were stationed in the primary schools. The Serb media glorified their army, saying that as long as they were there, we would be safe. If the Germans invaded, we would be protected. We never imagined these soldiers would soon start to kill *us*.

On a Monday, I went to Sanski Most to buy some clothes for school, and I ran into a young Serb teacher from my primary school. I hadn't seen him in three years. I didn't pay much attention to the red star on his hat, a symbol of rump Yugoslavia, mostly Serbia. I just thought he was part of the Yugoslav army. I was so happy to see him that I smiled and was about to speak when he said, "What are you doing in a Serb town?" I was shocked.

"What do you mean, a Serb town?" I asked. "This town is for everyone!"

"We'll see about that," he replied, and at that moment I realized he no longer saw me as human, but as his enemy. He was armed and looked as though he could kill me, and I was afraid. I couldn't believe my eyes. I didn't know what else to do, so I walked away. He had been my favorite teacher. I always wanted to be like him. He was an accordion player, too. I loved him, and now he saw himself as my enemy. When I think back on everything about Serbs from all of Yugoslavia killing us and what I went through, that day was the most difficult and the most damaging. Until then, we had all been living together in brotherhood and unity.

On my way back to the bus, I heard gunshots. I was too scared to look back and see what was happening. I just got on the bus and went back to my village. A few days later, we were watching TV and a news commentator reported that the Serbs had entered Sanski Most. We laughed, not believing this could actually be happening. Then our neighbor knocked on the door. "Come outside," he said. "You'll see." The sky above Sanski Most was light, tracer bullets were everywhere.

The Serbs had barricaded all the thoroughfares, and we couldn't get out. We hadn't stockpiled anything, so my sister tried to get to her house to get food. She came back screaming, "The Serbs have come. They're going to kill us." They had entered her village, destroyed houses, and killed *everyone* they encountered. Some people escaped to the forests and survived, but eventually they were turned in. The women were taken to concentration camps. Others were taken to a liberated territory in central Bosnia. My sister's Serbian friend called and told us to leave the village. "They're going to kill you," she said.

It happened so quickly I forgot to take anything with me. We went by bus to Prijedor, crossing all the barricades along the way, and got on another bus for Croatia. It was a long trip, and I felt a complete loss of control. At every border and barricade, armed men and soldiers stopped us and got on the bus. I prayed every minute that nothing would happen. I kept telling myself, "This can't be happening." This can happen in Palestine or Zimbabwe, but it cannot happen here. Luckily, I was fat and small, so I didn't look sixteen and they didn't bother with me. In truth, I wasn't worried about myself, I was worried about my sisters, my mother, and my nieces. My younger sister was an unmarried virgin, and for a Serb, that was like candy. I kept thinking, "What if something happens? How should I react?"

Forty-five minutes from the border of Croatia, a Chetnik soldier stopped us. [38] My mother told me to hide under my seat; she was afraid they were going to take me. But I was too big, and I knew it would be worse if he saw me hiding. When he got to us, he said, "Where are you going?" Right then, I realized that if I had to, I would kill him to defend my sister. In our religion, defending is different from aggressing, especially if a man needs to take care of his family. I knew if I looked at him in a way he didn't like, I could get killed, but I didn't care. It was more important to me to show him that we were human beings and we had a right to defend ourselves. All he said was, "You wanted Bosnia, but you will have hell." When he walked away, my mother passed out. She had already had two heart attacks; I thought she was having another one. "What if she dies here?" I thought.

We finally came to the Sana River border. There were only two boats going to Croatia. A soldier came to help me with my mother. I had already told my sisters to act as if they were separate from us, because they might take me away if they knew my mother had daughters who could help her. The soldier put us on the boat to cross the river. My sisters were on the same boat, but my mother, who had regained consciousness, and I pretended we didn't know them. That was the hardest part. I knew if we crossed the river, we would be safe. When we got across, a Croatian soldier, who was

---

[38] Chetnik fighters were Serbs who fought against the Axis powers during World War II. During the Bosnian genocide, they were committed to the creation of "Greater Serbia."

about nineteen, nodded to my mother. "What's wrong with her?" he asked me. "She fainted," I told him. "How old are you?" he asked. I told him "sixteen." "You don't look sixteen," he said. I didn't know what to say. I would have said anything just to get out of there. "Those motherfuckers don't have any power over you anymore," he said, nodding, and I knew we were safe.

In Croatia, we were still in the middle of a war zone, and when my mother regained consciousness, I could see she was really sick. I didn't know how to find an ambulance. There were planes overhead, and people were running everywhere trying to escape. Mother opened her eyes and looked at me, "Why are you worried?" she asked.

"Because of you," I said.

"I was just pretending," she said. I knew she just wanted me to feel okay. "We are free now," she said. "We are safe. Even if I die, it's fine. Just run away." She couldn't even walk.

Finally, I found a man with a van. We had about $200, and he took $100 to get us out of there. The siren was going off, which meant the danger was over for now, but everyone had to leave town because the Serbs could attack again. He took us to a place where we could wait for a bus to Zagreb. It was about five hours until the next bus came. As we were getting on the bus, another siren went off, which meant they were coming back to attack again. We had started at 4:00 in the morning, and now it was 5:00 that afternoon and we were on a bus to Zagreb, the capital of Croatia. It drove without lights. When we got to Zagreb, we called my father, who had stayed behind to take care of the house and the animals. He said he was sad he hadn't come with us, but that it was better this way since he thought the Serbs would come to the village soon and when they left, we could come home. We assumed we'd be back in a couple of weeks. We were gone for four years.

My mother's health was ruined for a time. She recovered after we got to Slovenia, where we stayed with my uncle. She felt safe until we got a phone call one night from my father. "This might be our last call," he told us. "They've started shelling." In the background, we could hear the bombs. My mother started crying. "Please take care of yourself," she told him. "Will you forgive me?" my father asked. In Bosnian custom, we ask for forgiveness if we know we are going to die. There are few people who are strong enough to ask for forgiveness. It's an acknowledgment of the end. My mother said, "What are you talking about? You'll be fine. I dreamed you will live.'"

That night, on Bosnian TV, they showed Serbs killing people in Sanski Most. Five days later, someone called us in Slovenia and told us they were killing people in our village. Within a half an hour, we heard that everyone in the village had been killed. We couldn't believe it. People we had known for years, our friends, neighbors, teachers, and doctors were all Serbs, and we did not understand how they could let them do this.

After three weeks, the first refugees from my village came to Slovenia, and they told us stories about who was killed and who had survived. My best friend had been killed. My mother's cousin lost fifteen members of her family. I went to see her, and we cried for hours. Finally, I was brave enough to ask, "Do you know where my father is?" She told me that she had seen a Chetnik carrying my father's identity card, saying he had killed him. I went home and tried not to talk about it. My mother asked, "Was your father killed?" she asked. "No," I said. I wanted her to live with hope.

After that, we were moved to a refugee camp in Slovenia, where I worked as an imam, teaching children and leading prayers. I did it for the people, not for God or myself. I couldn't find myself anymore. I had broken up with God because I didn't think He was fair. Life had lost meaning; it didn't make sense. When I slept, I had terrible nightmares, and when I was awake, I considered suicide. I thought it was the best way to escape. What kept me going was the thought that killing myself would be a victory for the Serbs. I didn't want to give them that.

Anger sustained me. I was so angry I didn't know what to do with it. I was angry at God, my mother, everyone! I didn't know why; I was just angry. I couldn't stand hearing my mother talk about when her husband would come home. After talking about him, she would say, "Inshallah." God willing. One day I told her to shut up. "He's dead. He won't come. Ever." "How do you know?" she asked. I told her I'd heard from her cousin. Within five days, my mother got diabetes. I wish I hadn't told her. She doesn't blame me for it now, but I still feel guilty that I told her. In the end, I think I saved myself.

I hated smoking and I hated other people smoking, but when we moved to the refugee camp in Slovenia, I started smoking. At a subconscious level, I think I was trying to kill myself. One night I was sitting outside, smoking and looking at the stars, and I felt so lonely. I was missing God very much. I don't remember when I first memorized prayers, but it felt as though I'd known them since I was born. Half of me was saying, "Make peace with God," and the other half disagreed: "He isn't fair. He let them do this to you. You're living like a dog in a refugee camp. You've lost everything." Before the war, I had everything I could have ever wanted. Now I didn't have a penny or, I felt, anything of value.

That night, the side that wanted to reconcile with God won. I accepted the poverty and that I'd lost everything. I accepted that I'd lost my father. I wasn't sure how, but I knew I had to start a new life—even though I wasn't sure that this was life. I wasn't sure about anything except that God was there, even if I didn't want Him to be. He was the only one who was there without my asking, and I started believing again. In traditional Islam, having a special relationship with God, one that nobody else has, is considered crazy. But I felt I did have a special relationship with God, and I felt a warmth around my heart. I knew I could betray Him, but He wouldn't betray me. This connection with God makes me what I am today.

On New Year's Eve, December 31, 1992, we got a phone call. There was only one phone in the refugee camp, and when my mother answered, she fainted. I was worried something had happened to my brother, so I took the phone. It was my father. He was alive! He said, "Honey, is that you?" I couldn't believe it. I said, "But you're dead." He said, "I'm not. I'll be with you before tonight." And he was. But he wasn't allowed in; the Slovenian authorities wouldn't give him refugee status. So he lived with his brother in Ljubljana and came to the gate every day to visit us. We hadn't seen him for eight months, and now we could only talk to him through the gate.[39]

In Slovenia, we were protected by the Geneva Conventions, which regulate the treatment of civilians, prisoners of war, and soldiers who are unable to fight. But the Slovenian authorities wouldn't let us do anything. The refugee camp leaders were Serbs, and all we were allowed to do was to sit around. "My God, look at me," I would think, "I don't do anything. I'm not worthy." It was torture.

To feel useful, I began teaching Arabic and English, even though my English was pretty bad. We lived in that prison till 1994. Then the government changed leadership, and we were allowed to have visitors and be educated. My theological high school wasn't recognized by the Slovenian authorities, so although I was twenty years old, I was still in the first grade. But I didn't mind. I just wanted to do something. When I wasn't in school, I counseled children who had lost family members. I couldn't trust adults because of the betrayal of my Serb teacher. The only people I trusted were children. They

---

[39] Vahidin was back in his traumatic adolescence as he told this part of his story. His speech was in short, clipped sentences. Although he told little of his process, this *was* his process. As a traumatized teenager, Vahidin experienced this very much the way he told it to me. Trauma speaks this way often, in short, clipped sentences, nearly breathless … as the experience was.

were innocent and wouldn't hurt anyone. I was extremely damaged, struggling to forgive the Serbs, but really I only wanted revenge. I believed they deserved to be punished. I wanted to kill them all, even their family members. No punishment would have sufficed.

We were put in a normal refugee camp in Slovenia, about 200 yards from the first one. As refugees, we were just numbers, not names. Whenever someone called me by my number, I would say my name out loud. They laughed, as though to say, "You poor little refugee. You can call yourself this name, but for me, you're just a number." Conditions weren't good, but even if I lived in a villa, the feeling that I was a refugee and couldn't provide for myself, earn money, or get a formal education was horrible. I spent my days reading books and dictionaries in English that people had left, and that's how I learned English.

But there was always the feeling of being a refugee. Before the war, we were in a position to help other people who weren't rich. We didn't have really poor people in our village, but there were people who had less than we did—gypsies or the elderly who had no children—and we would give to them. It was humiliating to be a refugee and have nothing to give. When my mother did our laundry at the camp, I had to cover myself in a blanket because I had no other clothes. An aid worker from an Italian humanitarian organization came to my room one laundry day and said, "Are you sick?" I said, "No, I don't have anything to wear." The next time she came, she brought me a nice sweater. I still have it. It was the first time I received something from somebody, and it was hard. It broke my pride. After that, I was able to receive, but I still had a bitter taste every time. I would think, "Will I be like this until I die?" The future was so unforeseeable, I didn't think we would ever return to Sanski Most.

Finally, in 1996, Sanski Most was liberated. My siblings stayed in Slovenia because it wasn't a war zone. My brother had lived there for a long time, so why not stay? But my parents and I wanted to return to Bosnia. I knew war might break out again, but I didn't care. I wanted to be myself, not a refugee. We heard there were a lot of murders at home, not just by Serbs, but by Mafia and other criminals, too. I went back to my sister's house, five minutes from our village. The Serbs had destroyed and rebuilt it three times. They fought among themselves about who would live in it because it was so beautiful. One Serb would live in it, and when he had to leave he would destroy it and say, "No one will live here." Then another Serb would rebuild it and live there. When he left, he would burn it. Then another Serb would rebuild it.

I could see our old house from the window at my sister's, but we couldn't go back yet because we didn't have the money to rebuild it. In my sister's house, the windows were still there, but there wasn't any of the same furniture. It didn't matter. It was the first time in four years and four months I had my own room. We stayed there for two years. Even though I started working in the school and became a teacher, which is a well-respected position, I was still a refugee in another village, and I thought of myself as such.

In the two years we lived at my sister's, my father rebuilt two rooms of our old house—the bathroom and the bedroom. It wasn't finished yet, but I wanted to move in. It was cold and we had no heater, but it was home. On March 8, 1998, still wintertime, I told my parents I couldn't stand being a refugee any longer and I wanted to move back into our house. They could wait for spring or summer, but I couldn't. Within minutes, we all agreed to return. A friend of ours, a volunteer from England, drove us there. Grass had grown over the roadways, and there was a tree growing right in front of the door. When I got out of the car, I performed gratitude prayers in front of the house and started crying. Our friend, who drove us said, "Don't cry, your house will be rebuilt." I told him, "I'm crying because I'm happy. I'm not a refugee anymore."

I wanted to scream, *"I'm not a refugee anymore!"* It was like taking off a suit of armor, a huge burden. I had my rights back!

That night we didn't have anything to cook on, so we made coffee at my uncle's house and brought it home. All we had was a toilet, a bed, and one big pillow. I slept on the pillow, and my parents slept in the bed. It was freezing, but it didn't matter. The feeling of being a refugee just melted away. Not long after, we held a funeral for the victims of my village. We took them from the mass graves, did the rituals, and reinterred them.

That's why I'm so connected to my house. I never want to live anywhere else. I hope God will give me that chance. I feel safe here. That's the main thing. I feel protected. No one can hurt me. My father hates that house. He rebuilt it, but he hates it. During the war, he was captured in front of the house by one of his friends, a Serb. So, he can't stand the house. He always encourages me to leave the village and live some-where else. But when I think about our house, I think of my mom and my beautiful childhood. I was safe, protected, and well-fed. I don't remember a minute of my childhood when I worried about anything. I had to complete eleven months of military service, but otherwise I stayed, working at the school teaching English.

One of the hardest things to deal with now is that we still see people who killed our parents, children, neighbors, and friends, and we're not allowed to say anything. A principal in one of the primary schools in Prijedor accused us of killing her husband. She called us a very derogatory name, and I felt rage. I told her that thirty-six people from my family were slaughtered. And friends, and friends of friends. I asked her, "Was your husband armed?" And she said, "Yes." I said, "Was it in another town?" And she said, "Yes, he was defending the Fatherland." Later, when I came to know Milka, my Serb friend, I found out that this woman was lying. Her husband had died in a car accident. She was a radical Serb, and that is how she became principal. Another Serb, a lady in my English class, said, "You're my neighbor. My uncle was a teacher who was captain of the Chetnik army." Her uncle was the one who ordered Chetniks to shell my village. I had to spend two months with this woman. Every time I looked at her, I thought two things: One, she loved him; and two, he was the Chetnik commander who ordered the shelling.

There are still people who have not returned and those whose bones have not been found. We don't know what happened to them. Every day we have to walk by a school director who was the commander when the school was turned into a concentration camp. He knows what happened to those people. He asks, "Why don't you say 'hello' to me?" and people tell him, "You were a Chetnik, the highest commander." And he says, "So what? I had to be." It's like a Nazi guard walking down the street in Israel. This goes on throughout Bosnia.

In Bosnia's schools, one is not allowed to say war criminal, war crime, Chetnik, or concentration camp. You can be jailed if you speak about it. In *Republika Srpska*, for example, it used to be normal for Serb TV newscasters to mention Bosniak holidays like the Day of Sorrow and the Day of Mourning, but in the last twelve years, they never mention such things. They erase history and create myths, such as that Karadžić is a hero. If you go to the market, you see his picture everywhere. Imagine how it feels for a Bosniak genocide survivor to go to Prijedor and see Karadžić's picture everywhere. Can you imagine seeing someone wearing a T-shirt with Hitler's picture on it?

My supervisor at school said, "There's an American professor coming to Sanski Most. Go and see what she's doing." I was excited to be exposed to someone from the West. But when he added that Serbs from Prijedor and Sanski Most would be there, too, I refused. I wouldn't sit with Serbs and talk to them. He said, "You have to go. If you don't, I'll fire you. I hired you, and I can fire you."

I did not want to sit down with Serbs because I did not want to feel the hatred. In the past, when I interacted with Serbs, they had a darkness in them I cannot explain. But as soon as I sat down at this gathering and looked at them, they looked so miserable, I felt, "I don't hate them. I feel sorry for them." And suddenly, I was glad I was a victim, rather than a victimizer. I realized I can live with nightmares of being chased or even killed, but what victims go through isn't as shameful as what perpetrators have to go through. Perpetrators have to face the fact that they caused tremendous suffering. To do this without hardening their hearts in self-defense against the victims' hatred and accusations must be next to impossible. Healing is harder for perpetrators than for victims. Victims merely have to tell their own truth.

One of the best things about Projekt Diacom was that I made friends with Milka, a Serb. Her friendship gave me strength. I realized, "You can't trust all Serbs, but you can trust some." During the project while I was processing those five years, Milka was very helpful. After Projekt Diacom, I was selected by Paula Green to come to the Training of Trainers group. I also participated in the CONTACT program at the School for International Training (SIT) in Vermont, where I met people from all over the world who had been through similar experiences. I completed the master's program at SIT in May 2003.[40]

---

[40] The CONTACT Summer Peacebuilding Program is a three-week professional and academic program in conflict transformation. The program takes place on the SIT Graduate Institute campus in Brattleboro, Vermont, where students learn about core ideas and practices in conflict transformation. See https://graduate.sit.edu/academics/certificate-programs/contact-summer-peacebuilding-program/

I learned to analyze myself and my culture. Hating Serbs and wanting revenge was one of the things that had kept me going, but at SIT, we had a class on forgiveness, and I learned about "burdening and unburdening." I love that term. To forgive means to unburden yourself and make your life easier. You don't forgive because the other person deserves it. You do it to unburden yourself. I did a lot of praying about this, and in the end, I succeeded. I forgave Serbs for what they did to me. I cannot do the forgiving for anyone else.

When Serbs say, "I'm sorry," they are saying it in the name of everyone. It also means, "I am guilty." From their point of view, if I say, "I forgive," it means that I forgive them in the name of everybody. But I can forgive them only for myself and for what they did to me. What I'm forgiving is not important anymore. I'm forgiving in order to unburden myself. Since I forgave, my life has been easier. I don't have that rage in my heart, the anger or bitterness I had before.

I even see colors in a new way. Before the war, I saw colors as bright, vivid, and beautiful. During and after the war, my bitterness didn't let me enjoy things, and I literally could not see colors. Everything was gray. I couldn't even enjoy my mother's presence, and she is my best friend. I didn't enjoy anything, except for children. From 1992 until 2000, my heart was sick. If I went into nature, I couldn't enjoy it. Now it looks beautiful again! From time to time I still feel angry, but I can do something about it now. After I unburdened, I thought I'd never be angry again. No one told me, "You will, but there's nothing strange about it. You may get angry or cry, and it will be hard to tell your story over and over. It will be hard for you to see Serbs as your friends, but seeing them as your friends is not a prerequisite of healing." I was lucky to have Sorija, a Serb who had the same opinion I did about a lot of things, and a Serb friend from Banja Luka, and Milka.

Through this healing, I've learned that we can do anything we want to. When I went to Switzerland to a peace camp with the Israelis and Palestinians, a man asked me,

"What do you need to remain in Bosnia to do this work?" I said 400 Euros, and he gave it to me. It was amazing. Now I'm my own boss. I create my own time. I do projects I love. God has been generous and gracious. I believe that God will sustain this project, no matter how hard it is.

I want to build a Center for Peacebuilding in my village.[41] I want to bring Serbs here to interact with the people. Many of them don't want to know Serbs. I don't blame them, but I want them to be exposed to just one nice Serb. When I say nice, I mean someone who doesn't admire Karadžić, someone like Milka. Then they might see that they don't have to hate Serbs. That's how I came to this. When I tell people I want to build a peace center, they think I'm crazy. I need money and human resources. But God will take care of the funding, I'm sure of it.

Spirituality is an important part of reconciliation. It is God who gave me the desire, the will to live and to search for healing. We were lucky to have ten of us sitting in the same circle, even if we didn't have the same opinions about things. We were listening to one another. If it hadn't been Projekt Diacom, something else would have helped me. I was lucky to have Paula, my guardian angel. She helped me get to where I am today. Without her, it would have been much harder. I might have had to wait another twenty years before someone said, "You can do this." Yet without my faith, I don't think I could have been this honest with her or any of the Projekt Diacom people, or even with the idea of Projekt Diacom. When we start reconciliation and healing, it's important to begin with prayer, whether we pray in a traditional or an updated way. Prayer brings courage. Because we feel supported, we know we can do it. If you and I are spiritual,

---

[41] When Vahidin and I spoke in July 2010, he had accomplished this dream. He now dreams of founding a peace embassy.

we already share something and can talk from a common place.

It's important that we and the Serbs start dialoguing about something we can agree on, such as the time we spent as Communists. If we say, "That was bad," everyone agrees. And if we say, "In a sense, it was also good," they also agree. If we are from Sanski Most, we might say, "The River Sana is so beautiful; we should protect it." They will agree, and we can talk about the river and how we're so proud of it. "It was always the most beautiful river on Earth," someone might say, "even in '92 when human bodies were floating in it." There will be silence, and the facilitator might say, "Do you want to say something about that?" Then the dialogue begins, and you hear five different truths from five people. It doesn't matter who they are or even what they say, only that the truth is being told.

These are the types of workshops I'm leading now. I continue this work because I want others to experience what I've experienced. I want people to read about it and become interested. If they have problems, I want them to ask for help. We all need help. Culturally, we are taught not to see therapists. If we do, we are considered crazy and we can't get married or lead a normal life. But everyone needs to visit a therapist. I have heard people calling this "recovery," but for me, *healing* is a good word. Without healing, on both an individual and collective level, we will have another war. If we have healing, war may be prevented.

The Serbs' healing depends on us. I don't think they can heal without us. One Serb told me he has nightmares every night, that he hasn't slept since the war stopped. I think he wanted me to say, "I'm sorry," but instead I said, "I'm glad to hear that. I can't help you get over your nightmares, but I'm so glad Serb soldiers have nightmares that will make you come to me saying, 'Look, can you help me?'" It showed me he has a conscience. So we dialogued, and now he hardly has nightmares. If they are not aware of what they did, if they don't acknowledge what they did, they will kill us again. They have the power to do that.

When Paula was talking about her experiences with Israelis and Palestinians, she said, "If we don't deal with things from the past, our children will have to do it." If I go through trauma, I'm the one that needs to heal from it, so my children and the children of these Serbs don't have to. But the Serbs' healing process will take longer than ours because they must be ashamed. Not necessarily this generation, because they might not see it. The real changes will probably happen within the next generation, if the present generation doesn't make another war.

I no longer think Serbs should be killed because I'm coming from a deeper place. If I were just a Bosniak, I would say they should be killed; they betrayed us. My core issue is not about them killing our neighbors and students and raping our grandmothers. It's about betrayal, the fact that they betrayed people who loved and trusted them.

Today in Sanski Most, people get married and are quickly divorced. When I ask why, they say, "Because he betrayed me." People were betrayed at such a deep level it's too easy for them to feel betrayed again. Every time I do workshops with Bosnians, I make this point. We feel betrayed by Serbs and by everybody, even internationally. Islamic countries, our brothers and sisters according to faith, did almost nothing for us, especially Saudi Arabia, where the holy cities, Mecca and Medina, are. People sent money from there, but that wasn't enough.

We're all in this together. If you're hungry, I will not just give you lunch today and say goodbye. How do I know you're not going to be hungry tomorrow? As human beings, we're responsible for each other. I didn't think this way before the war. I didn't care what was going on out there. I was sorry that people were getting killed, but I felt it was up to them; they should take care of it. Now I understand differently.

We live in Europe, and Europe doesn't understand or even tolerate Muslims and Islam. Europeans are afraid of us. Their fear is making some Bosnian Muslims convert to radical Islam. Because Europeans fear Muslims, they are getting the worst variety of it. Soon we will have al-Qaeda Muslims in Bosnia, which will be the excuse the Serbs need to finish the genocide. I pray this won't happen, but as long as the international community prohibits us from speaking about these atrocities, it can happen again.

The Dayton Accords aren't about peace. They're about the absence of war. In Dayton, we just solidified things as they were at the moment. The Serbs still have Serbia behind them, and they want half of Bosnia, too. If someone kills one person because of their nationality, then it's a Holocaust, and this Holocaust is still happening here, unspoken, but happening. I'd like to be optimistic, but if the situation continues in this direction, may God help us.

The advice I'd give someone who has gone through genocide is, "Don't give up. Don't let anyone from either side discourage you from coming all the way through." I was discouraged many times. I held a peace camp with Serbs from Republika Srpska, and we became close friends. Three years later, we had another peace camp in Republika Srpska. The first day, one of these friends told me, "Be aware. You're in Republika Srpska. This is not your land."

I felt like giving up, but I didn't. Don't let cowards discourage you from reaching your goal. Being healed is like escaping from a hole. You're free. There is light. Going through all the pain you have to get here is worth it. Trust God and trust people. Without people, I wouldn't be where I am today. Without Serbs, I wouldn't have healed.

*"The soul is healed by being with children."*
— Fyodor Dostoyevsky

# Chapter 4
# Milka Marinković
# Humility

*"If I could regain my integrity, I would be able
to look to the future with more hope."*

In the summer of 2003, on the last day of the Karuna
Center for Peacebuilding's dialogue project, Milka Marinković (Mílk-uh Mar-ínk-o-vitch) sat in a hard, wooden chair,
leaned forward, and hugged her new American soccer ball to
her chest. One of the Karuna Center's sponsors had sent
soccer balls for all the participants, and we had just distributed
them. Milka's midlength, straight, dark hair matched her
downcast yet glistening brown eyes. In a quiet, trembling
voice, she expressed gratitude for the dialogue project and
said she would never forget Paula or any of us. As a Serb in
the recent war, even though she was completely innocent of
any misdeeds, Milka blamed herself for not doing anything
to stop the war.

In the early stages of the dialogue project, Muslims sat apart from the Serbs. Bosniaks did not trust Serbs and didn't want to socialize with them. Some Serbs and Muslims had known each other before the war, which made this dynamic even more awkward and tense.

As time went on, because of Milka's honesty and remorse, Vahidin came to trust her, and the two became friends. They sat together at meals, laughing, huddling, and talking. Milka was the one Serb in the group Vahidin trusted because she told the truth and suffered *consciously* for her group's actions during the war.[42]

My interview with Milka took place in a hotel in Prijedor,[43] her home city. Her voice was muted, her gaze often lowered. This demeanor may have been due in part to her innate modesty, but it might also speak of ongoing shame. The centerpost of humility, or contrition, for Milka seemed appropriate due to her regret that she hadn't done more to stop the war. Because of her humility, vulnerability, and regret, Milka became an important bridge between the Bosniaks and Serbs in the Karuna Center training, and a significant figure in Vahidin's healing from hatred and color blindness.

*Here is Milka Marinković, in her own words:*
When I was young, we lived under Communism in one Yugoslavia. My life was filled with friends, colleagues, and relatives of all ethnicities. We shared a unity and a brother-hood. If I had faith in anything, it was that. We believed in the home and the progressive nature of education, and we

---

[42] See Lynn McTaggert, *The Bond: Connecting Through the Space Between Us.* (New York, Free Press, 2001), 115: "We are not prompted to help others when we imagine ourselves in their situation. Rather, we act on our natural compassion when we can tune into another person's feelings, *move beyond the sense of self, and take the other's perspective.*"

[43] See the next chapter for an explanation of Prijedor.

were proud of our land. I was stronger then, and life seemed more engaging. Now I feel I was cheated out of that life.

Under Socialism, we had a one-party system. After that, we had adopted a multiparty system, and Serbs, Muslims, and Croats each formed their own nationalistic party. Under the multiparty system, the campaign rhetoric became aggressive, using the language of hatred and revenge. Politicians tried to convince us that Yugoslavia's past had been awful and that unity and brotherhood never really existed. I was amazed by the increase in hatred. The ideals of my youth suddenly fell away, and I began to wonder if I'd made a mistake believing in unity and brotherhood.

Serbs began to think that whoever wasn't with them was against them. Suddenly, our jobs were in question, and since we needed jobs to survive, we went along with the rising tide of nationalism. I knew it wasn't right, but I thought that intellectuals and others in high positions would help the people come to their senses. I was wrong about that.

Elections were held in 1990, and the war started in 1992. For those two years, there was a false peace. Uniformed soldiers walked the streets; men and boys who had never served in the army before became commanders. When the war started, houses were looted and burned, women were raped, and later I learned that people were tortured. On the way to my grandfather's house one day, I passed through a familiar village. All the houses had been shelled. Cattle were wandering around without food or water. It was horrible.

War was never declared, so the international community considered it a civil war. By misnaming it, they were able to dismiss it. Local TV and radio announced that we were *liberating* part of the country. I didn't know what to think. One night, the local news ran stories how insurgents had surrounded Prijedor to defend it. There was a lot of killing on both sides. My Serb neighbor was killed by a sniper. The officials said the sniper was a Bosniak, but no one knew, and it was dangerous to doubt what we were told. When a Bosniak was killed, they justified it by saying he owned a radio station or had a weapon. They vilified him. In some cases, I knew the person and knew it wasn't true, but I was too intimidated to say anything. Educated people also spouted nationalistic ideas. Well-intentioned people convinced me to stay quiet, saying, "You have a child. Don't speak our way or your child will be in danger."[44]

Refugee camps started to pop up everywhere. No one used the words "death camps" or "concentration camps," but that's what they were. People were concentrated in one place and not allowed to go anywhere. We were told people were taken to these camps for questioning. They said that Keraterm[45] was not a death camp, but a collection camp, a gathering of people. Even if these people were just being detained, that alone was humiliating. I felt horrible when I saw men's wives bringing them food, and yet I was afraid to say "good morning" or "good evening" to the guards.

In a camp near me, women with children were collected. From there they went to third countries, like Germany or Serbia or somewhere not of their origin. In a way I envied the people who were in a prison camp and then were sent away. I was on the outside. Anything could happen to me. I felt worse being on the "safe" side of the barrier. Every time I passed by a camp I felt guilty, but I couldn't talk about it to anyone. The men were taken to Omarska Camp, where most

---

[44] By "our way," Milka meant the Serb way, whereas Marijana (chapter 6) speaks of not being able to speak "her way" either, a Croat way. Before the war, anyone could speak any way they wanted. The dialects are very similar.

[45] In two of the concentration camps during the Bosnian Genocide, Omarska and Keraterm, killings, torture, and brutal interrogations were carried out. The third, Trnopolje, was a staging area for massive deportations, mostly of women, children, and elderly men. Killings and rapes also took place there. A fourth, Manjaca, was referred to by Bosnian Serbs as a prisoner-of-war camp, although most if not all detainees were civilians. The Commission of Experts determined that the systematic destruction of the Bosniak community in the Prijedor area met the definition of genocide.

people didn't survive. Non-Serbs plundered and "cleansed" the villages these Serbs had to leave behind. Pillaging and plundering were done by people on all sides, though by far the greatest part of it was done by my own ethnicity, the Serbs. Most people in Bosnia-Herzegovina who participated in extermination of each other saw in it their chance to seize somebody else's property. In Prijedor, Serbs seized Bosniaks' property. In Sanski Most, Serbs seized Bosniaks' property, and then Bosniaks seized Serbs' property. And in Zenica, the Bosniaks did it. Zenica is where my brother's family was relocated. Everywhere, people were taking others' houses.

When my son and I went to see my mother, she would say, "This will pass. Every evil will pass. It won't last long." During World War II, she had lost a son, and she had told her other two sons to be careful, not to do evil things, just survive. My mother told me to keep my bags packed. We Serb villagers were always afraid, so we always had our things packed. If anyone attacked us, we'd be ready to leave. Wondering whether we might have to go on short notice was a way to keep us afraid. One of my brothers was living in Croatia, one was in Zenica, and one was here in Prijedor, which is now in the Serb part of Bosnia. They had secure jobs, but they couldn't get sick because they had a "working obligation." They had to be there every day.

In August 1992, the patriarch of the Serbian Orthodox Church, Pavle, made an announcement that it was time to repent. He said, "There is no benefit to God, to the church, nor to the family that could free us from the obligation to be human beings and to behave as human beings." His announcement was a ray of light in the darkness. I hoped it would make an impression on the people. I kept praying that people would be ashamed of what they were doing, but it didn't make any difference. It wasn't a turning point, because overall, the church was supporting nationalism.

I am an Orthodox Christian, but not a believer. I only pray in really difficult situations, for example if my child were

71

in danger. My father was an atheist. We both supported my mother in her faith because it was such a comfort to her. So I can't say much about faith, except that spirituality can be a solace for people. I don't think religion should ever be imposed on others as it was during the war. Before the war, priests and the church were not active. When the war came, the priests began to influence people toward patriotism. They talked about love and compassion, but their actions were the opposite. They never explicitly taught hatred, but hatred was always between the lines. The church used religion for political purposes by engaging in propaganda that encouraged believers to support government policy.

It was a time when civilization had no rules, when the living envied the dead. I thought I would never be normal again. I felt hopeless. I was just a plant, a vegetable, a being who lives, nothing else. I had a child, and I was working with young students, and perhaps that's why I started to feel angry at myself for not doing anything to stop the war. Anger can be useful. It made me stronger. I knew I'd never be this naïve again.

I divided people into three groups: those who didn't do anything, who were passive; those who changed themselves overnight into people who could kill; and those who transformed themselves positively. The third group didn't exist in Bosnia at the time. The only exception might be the Seventh Day Adventists. Their priests fed the children and helped everyone. Other nongovernmental organizations (NGOs) were front groups for nationalists. The president of the Red Cross in Bosnia, for example, was the wife of Karadžić, so it was actually a cover for Serb nationalism.[46]

---

[46] In my final interview with Milka, she said she hadn't made the comment about Karadžić's wife and the Red Cross. Perhaps one of the translators said it. The information is accurate according to the BBC. See http://news.bbc.co.uk/2/hi/europe/2571579.stm

I felt very alone during this time. I didn't have much materially, no electricity or even the basics to live. This was one of the ways the Serb nationalist government used to wear us down, depriving us of our basic needs. We were also very isolated from one another. If there were others with a similar outlook, we were separated and afraid to talk. Only after the Dayton Accords did we start to ask ourselves who we are and what we could do now. We Serbs who survived the last decade of the last century will never be able to trust our nation again. We burned from the inside, from the pain and injustice. We lost something essential. By the time the war ended, I had not suffered any personal losses. My brother, who lived in Croatia died of natural causes in 2000. I lost my mother, too, so I understood the feeling of loss, but not like those whose family members were murdered. I suffered, but not in the way those who were tortured did. The worst for me is that my son was traumatized because he didn't have a good childhood, and this period cannot be restored.

A group of women in our neighborhood organized to do something, but we didn't know what to do. Around that time, Paula Green began working with groups of Serb and Muslim women in Prijedor. I went to the first meeting and wrote down what she said: "It is enough just to imagine something, and then our life will be created out of that. But," she added, "to create this life, Serbs have to acknowledge what they did." Paula insisted that truth was a necessary step toward reconciliation. She had passed through hard times herself. That helped us accept ourselves.

Paula and her team had a difficult time convincing people that they must acknowledge and tell the truth. We had to go through the process slowly. We didn't make progress as a group, but we did make progress individually. Paula taught us to trust that coexistence would be possible again. She gave us hope.

In her seminars, I realized that telling the truth is possible. But it's hard, and I'm still worried it won't happen in the way it needs to. People are afraid to speak up because of educational and cultural barriers that make us feel we can't. Others don't think it's necessary to speak up, or else they worry they will say the truth and the people around them won't support them. I told the truth, and now a lot of people treat me like a traitor. We have to change the climate so that we can trust one another again. The authority of those who speak can mean a lot to others trying to learn. People can be healed simply by speaking the truth, but because we were so suppressed, we need permission from someone in authority to speak the truth.

In our part of the world, we have cycles of peace and war. Even when there is peace, it's preparation for another war. If we could influence the people who committed the atrocities and simultaneously heal the war criminals, we might be able to heal as a whole and stop this cycle of violence. *Healing* means getting back what we have lost. We can only do that if others around us are healed, too. We cannot be healed alone. We can't feel well if those around us are sick. *No man is an island.*[47] By expressing our truth and our integrity, it can help the people around us and then spread throughout Bosnia and the whole region and give everyone courage.

All three nations in Bosnia-Herzegovina—Bosnian Muslims (Bosniaks), Bosnian Serbs, and Bosnian Croats— need to reenvision history. Presently, each nation has a story justifying its actions and its position. We need one story. I would like to believe it's possible. A reform in education is underway, and it's moving in that direction. President Čavić of Republika Srpska admitted for the first time in public that the moment of truth about the atrocities in Srebrenica had come. He did not try to diminish what happened. In a

---

[47] Though most of Milka's interview was in Bosnian, translated into English, she spoke this sentence in English, for emphasis.

preliminary statement, he said the atrocities were unimaginable, pointing out that only truth can lead to sincere reconciliation and coexistence. In the past, the Republika Srpska denied everything, but they cannot deny it anymore. I did not hear anyone call him a traitor.

Young people want to hear their elders' stories. They want to resolve problems in a new way. They want to be armed with understanding and turn out better than their parents did in this war. We who have experienced war want to make sure that young people know that war is not about heroism or courage, nationalism or anything. If we can educate the younger generation about the atrocities of war, I feel more confident we won't have another war.

I use every opportunity to teach the young conflict resolution. I am actively trying to spread peace and hope to the children, their parents, and teachers. Visitors are astonished to witness children learning peacebuilding at the centers led by NGOs. I am teaching democracy to twelve and thirteen year olds. I teach what I learned in Paula's class about the cycle of violence. It's a civil rights class, and the topic is peace. The children cut out newspaper articles or papers they prepare from watching TV, explain why peace is important and why it needs to be taught in the schools. Then they present their work to the community. People come from all over and are impressed by how the children are learning peace.

If we could prevent the next generation from starting another war, we might be able to recover our integrity and authenticity. If I can regain my integrity, I will be able look to the future with hope. I am still caught by fear. I don't think anyone has really recovered, but individually and collectively, we need to make every effort to restore the norms of civilization. We need to help each other during our healing process and never let such evil spread again.

slab outdoors for a day or maybe two in baking heat. Two inmates managed to pull him inside, and he was screaming from the pain of a broken arm. An inmate set his arm, but by that time, they said my husband had turned dark blue. After about a week, two soldiers came into the room during the night and told my husband to come with them. My brother was also in that large dorm room at the time. The people heard two car doors slamming, so it must have been a two-door sedan, not a large car, that came to take him away. That's the last anyone ever heard of him.

I was very angry, but no one would talk about what happened. So I did whatever I could to go on with my children, and somehow, I managed. My mother-in-law said, "The dear Lord created this," and I thought, "If there's a God, He would *not* have made this." It's fundamental to Islam to stay calm and not get angry, but to be patient and endure. She told me not to cry. "If you cry and he's still alive, it does no good," she said. Although Islam believes people should insist on truth, in most Muslim families, there was no talk about what happened.

The majority of Serbs also don't talk about the past, but Serbian children hear about their oppression by the Ottoman Turks from a young age. In their schools, the children are taught that Serbs have been victimized throughout history, and their stories are filled with acts of vengeance. Bosnian Muslim children never hear about wars that way or talk about it in their families. I had a healthier childhood because I did not hear these kinds of stories. In the 1990s, the media, which was controlled by Milošević, told the Serbs that we wanted a jihad against them, and many were afraid to talk to us Muslims. Fear makes us vulnerable to manipulation. When Serbs sought revenge against Muslims, they were thinking of fourteenth-century Turks. Milošević promised the Serbs a small war, like taking back a car someone has stolen from you. But it was a huge war, and it was about ancient revenge.

It continues to repeat itself. Serbia doesn't want to recognize Bosnia-Herzegovina as a whole country. They want Republika Srpska to be part of Serbia. They cannot change this because of the Dayton Accords, but I'm afraid in fifty years we'll have another war. The Bosnian Serbs have one history and the Bosnian Muslims another. This can make for war. We need to teach children about tolerance, peacebuilding, and nonviolence. We need to make a new history together.

After the bomb exploded in my house, we were taken to Zagreb, Croatia, in a convoy organized for Bosniaks from Prijedor. My parents were already there as refugees. I began to lose hope of finding my husband, or at least finding him quickly. We were taken by the United Nations High Commissioner for Refugees (UNHCR)[50] into political asylum in Denmark, where I was recognized as a refugee. I got a job, and my daughter went back to school. But after the Dayton Accords were signed, I wanted to return to Bosnia to continue looking for my husband. There were reports that some inmates in concentration camps were still alive. So we went back to search. I held onto that hope for years. It was hard to let go. Because there are so many who witnessed what happened to my husband and because he was such an important person, his case is among the testimonies at The Hague.

Later, after we gave up hope of his return, as a family we still wanted to find his body to give him a proper burial. We felt that would bring us peace. The love of my children and my husband has been the central organizing principle of my life, my foundation. Living for others and providing an example for them has sustained me. I don't think I could have done it as well without Paula Green. I feel sorry for everyone

---

[50] The office of the UN High Commissioner for Refugees (UNHCR) was created in 1950, in the aftermath of World War II, to help millions of Europeans who had fled or lost their homes. The organization continues to protect and assist refugees around the world.

who didn't meet her and go through these seminars, including my children. She helped me understand what happened, learn to cooperate with Serbs again, and do inner work on my own trauma. I know she had a hard time too, and that helped me as well.

I keep thinking what a good person my husband was and how what happened to him is not fair. My children have the same thoughts. Sometimes we can hardly cope. In the face of such awful circumstances, you need reasons to go on living. For instance, my son believes his father would be happy if he finishes his studies, so his goal is to complete his studies and return to Prijedor to work as a dentist. My husband loved that I looked nice, so I keep investing in my appearance. I can't imagine going through Prijedor not wearing nice clothes, not being presentable. When I feel depressed and tired, the thought of him saying, "You look so nice," keeps me going, keeps up my sense of pride. I work with children who went through what mine did, because I want to do more than just survive. I want to act. When you are active, you think less about the things that brought you to the place where you are. I want to show others that it is possible to go through war and survive it.

To me, the definition of recovery is to come to a place where you understand what happened and feel strong enough to go on. You learn to live with uncertainty and pain. Paula helped me do this. Without her, I would still be depressed, probably on sedatives, and my children wouldn't have a strong mother they can look up to.

Radmilla was one of the Serb women in Projekt Diacom. The first time, Paula put Radmilla and me face-to-face, it was awkward and tense. I could hardly look at her. We had worked together at the same school. She was the principal, and we had been friends. Then I was fired from the school, and

Radmilla stopped communicating with me. She never phoned. The same thing happened to other colleagues and friends, because even the Serbs closest to us (some were godparents to our children) called us extremists, even though until then we had spent most of our time together.

At the workshop, Radmilla commented how "hard" it must have been for me to "leave" my home. I was infuriated, and I told her in front of the whole group I hadn't *chosen* to leave my home. I was expelled! We were ethnically cleansed! This minimization, this denial of our situation drove me crazy. But after saying this, I felt free, and closer to Radmilla. This is the power of truth. After you tell the truth and are heard and accepted, it becomes easier to face what happened and what might happen in the future. After each Karuna Center seminar, I felt stronger. The work was exhausting and difficult, and I had to drop my pride and cry a lot. In my culture and in my family, we don't cry or express our feelings openly. I felt I should be strong. But with Paula and the people in Projekt Diacom, I felt protected. Paula heard what I was saying, and she would nod, and I knew I was in a safe place.

That session was my turning point. I knew after that I could go on my own. I could become part of the reconciliation process. I could talk about what happened without crying. I could speak face to face with Radmilla, and for the first time, I could say how I felt. I felt strong enough to insist on truth. My children need me to be both mother and father, and I do my best in each role. I think I'm better at it because I went through the process of Projekt Diacom. I feel satisfied that my children don't hate anyone.

By chance, I encountered the man who ordered my husband out of our house and even hit him on his way out. I told him one sentence that he said to my husband when he was taken to Omarska. The man was astonished that I knew what he had said because I never saw my husband after he was captured. He was even more astonished that I didn't hate him at that moment. I felt strength being able to tell him that, even years later. Surely now his conscience is haunting him.

I am ready to forgive because I don't know what it is to hate. I cannot imagine teaching my children to hate or to get revenge, and I don't feel that way either. Nothing can make me ashamed. I feel proud that I was married to my husband. They all knew him and thought well of him. I suppose the person who killed him has been having a hard time for many years. I may never feel completely safe again, knowing there are people who beat and kill people. Many of the people who did these horrible things are still alive, and we haven't yet healed as a community. We are not yet open with one another, individual to individual, community to community, and facing what happened is not easy. Lies continue, events are exaggerated, everyone has a version of the story that suits them. In Bosnia, we are repeating stories from the Second World War that simply aren't true. We need to get to the point where everyone shares the same story, the same understanding of what happened. We need the same truth, or we will have another war fighting over who was "right" and who was "wrong" in the last one.

I would advise people who are suffering from the horrors of war to go through something like Projekt Diacom, where they will be encouraged to understand the other person's position and to work on themselves. It's a kind of therapy. I advise everyone to think positively but always tell the truth. It is possible to both survive and keep one's dignity.

# The Clinicians from
## Clinica Medica in Zenica
# Sabiha Husić and Marijana Senjak

Sabiha Husić and Marijana Senjak were colleagues who worked together at the Clinica Medica (Medical Clinic) in Zenica, an industrial city in central Bosnia, at the time of the interviews. Sabiha is a practicing Bosnian Muslim theologian and a social worker. Marijana is a Croat psychologist who lived in Bosnia at the time of the war. These two clinicians and the clinic itself played a crucial role in the lives of rape survivors and their babies during the war.

*"Our prime purpose in life is to help others."*
— The Dalai Lama

# Chapter 6
# Sabiha Husić
# Faith

*"My religion is my life. It helps me live more easily."*

Warmth radiates from Sabiha Husić (Sa-bée-ha Hú–sich) like a wood-burning stove on a bleak winter's day. To me, Sabiha is an open channel for the divine to pass through and bless others. At the time of our initial interview, she and Marijana greeted Lutvija and Vesna (our translators), my brother Dan and me with fresh mint tea and honey accompanied by vanilla cookies she'd baked that morning. Delicate scents were wafting in the air with this warm welcome. At the same time, an almost haunted look of residual suffering and great depths of feeling showed in Sabiha's intense eyes, giving, as in Senka's case, an almost opposite impression from the radiancy and warmth she projected. This, I found, is the haunted look of trauma.

Of Sabiha's many virtues—which include modesty, self-transcendence, integrity, altruism, and bravery—she made it clear that it was her *faith* in God that sustained her during her darkest days, pointing her away from the pain inside herself and toward helping others. Sabiha was able to feel gratitude even as she suffered through one of several of the worst atrocities of the last century. In spite of her suffering and that of her people, she still thinks forgiveness is crucial to recovery. Though some interviewees in this book do not emphasize forgiveness, for Sabiha it was indispensable to her healing. She was able to forgive those who had committed atrocities during the war because of her faith.

*Here is Sabiha Husić, in her own words:*
In 1992, I was a second-year student in the School of Theology in Predna, Montenegro, a beautiful Balkan country that borders Bosnia. I spent the month of Ramadan fasting and doing spiritual practices and planned to return to the Islamic University in Sarajevo afterward. But two days after Ramadan, war broke out in Bosnia-Herzegovina, and we Muslims were detained in Predna. During the six months I stayed there, it was extremely difficult to contact my parents. I realized that even in wartime, I needed to return to my family in Vitez village, near Zenica, Bosnia-Herzegovina, but I didn't have a passport.

Before the war, we didn't need passports. We used identity cards to go to other countries. Then Macedonia passed a law that Bosnians could not enter without a passport, and although Macedonia shares a border with Bosnia, to get back home I had to pass through Macedonia, and I could not get there without a passport. It took me three tries to get into Macedonia; finally, some people helped me. In Macedonia, people thought I was insane for wanting to go to Bosnia, but I didn't really believe there was a war. (This attitude was typical of many Bosniaks.) So I traveled through Bulgaria,

Romania, and Croatia to get home. In each country, I had to face the identity card issue.

It took me twenty-one days to get from Montenegro to Bosnia. Normally it's a day trip. The telephones weren't working, so I couldn't call my parents along the way. My friends in Zagreb, Croatia, helped me buy tickets to Travnik in Bosnia, where I could get a taxi to Vitez, my village. I had no money but figured that when I got to my parents, they would help me. In the taxi, I asked the driver if he knew my parents. He said he did. He wanted to know why I asked. I told him it was dangerous to travel with someone we didn't know and I was being cautious. When I got to my parents' house, my brother was the first to come out. Everyone was in shock to see me; they couldn't believe I had come home.

I lived at home with my parents for about three months, and then war broke out in Vitez on April 6, 1992. It was horrible. Overnight, it was a war zone. Until then, relations among the ethnic groups were good. The morning that war came to our village, my father was getting ready for work. He stayed home, waiting to see what would happen. It was really dangerous. People were getting killed in front of our house! Our closest neighbors were Croats, and they helped us. One came to our house and asked my father and mother to come out of the house. He promised to help my father get safely to other Croatians.[51] Even though my father was eventually wounded by Croatian snipers, this Croatian neighbor helped him escape.

On the sixth day of the fighting in Vitez, we decided to flee. We tried to get help from the UN stationed near Vitez, but they couldn't or wouldn't help us. We finally left at three in the morning with a small group of other people, including

---

[51] Bosnians use both words "Croat" and "Croatian" as an adjective and a noun. I quote Sabiha as she said it here. The words seemed interchangeable to me in usage, although a dictionary may distinguish them from one another.

young women and small girls. En route to Travnik, we were stopped by Croats, so for three days, we hid in a field. To stay alive, we had to scatter, so my mother went to one side of the field and I to another. For three weeks, she and I crossed different mountains and took different routes. When we finally got to Zenica, we were given refugee status. Every community had a branch that helped refugees, and because my father was a Serb, we were given a Serbian house to stay in. After that, we were given another Serbian house and told we could live there the rest of our lives. That's when I finally let in that there really was a war going on in Bosnia.

Everything in Zenica was new to us. We had no tradition here. My parents were in the house, but the things in the house weren't ours. We would sit around, and none of us would speak. We thought we'd be able to return to our house in seven or eight days, but almost immediately we heard that our house had been burned down and the residents of Vitez were being killed.

I had a good father. He raised us with love and taught us that hatred never yields a positive result. Through him, I started the work I do now. During the war, my father was wounded and near death. Two of my brothers were captured, first by the Croatian side and then by the Serbian side. When war broke out, my brother's wife went with their daughter to stay with her family near Novabilja, between Travnik and Vitez. It was a long time before my brother saw his wife and daughter again. When he tried to see them, a Croatian soldier captured him, and he spent three months in Banja Luka.

We lived near the refugee camp. I was still young. Before the war I had only one task: to study at the university. Now, I needed a new reason to live, so I asked my family if we could make our house a gathering place for refugees. I organized meetings for women and girls, and every day we'd spend a few hours talking together. We used humor, and some of them suggested it was important to begin the meetings with prayer. So we included prayers for peace, for the house, and for those who were wounded and killed. After a while, we began to talk about what was happening to us—how we were sleeping, where we spent our time during the day, and so on. Some of them wanted me to teach the Islamic religion. Before the war, everyone lived openly. Some practiced religion, and some didn't. During the war, a lot of people felt let down by organized religion, but they still had a relationship with God. They told me, "When the war started, only God helped me."

One woman had been raped in front of her six-year-old daughter at their house near Vitez. She told me, "I didn't cry because I didn't want to cry in front of my daughter." Her daughter recited a simple prayer, "Oh God, please help me make it easier for Mommy, and not so complicated. ... Oh God, give us good." This was based on the first prayer Muslim people learn. After hearing this, the woman told me she felt confidence and strength in herself. She said, "I started to believe I would survive."

That woman wanted to talk about religion. She'd never practiced religion before the war; she had been an atheist. But prayer helped her, and she wanted to learn more. A lot of women wanted to learn about and practice religion because they found safety and security in it. It helped them accept their experiences, and it connected them with others. In Islam, we are taught not to hate people. When I worked with one woman, I asked if she hated her rapist. She said she didn't, nor did she feel that punishment would change him or help her forget what happened. She believed God would give the perpetrators what they deserved. Only God knew what happened to her during that period, and she believed God would punish him. Faith can be important for women's healing. It can free them of negative attitudes.

This woman invited me to Medica, the clinic in Zenica, to see how they worked. I began to visit women in different villages around Zenica. I knew a lot of families, and I included them in my social field work. As a theologian, I had the advantage of being able to visit Muslim families and speak

with them about things they don't usually talk about. At first,
I visited the families as a whole. After we established a good
connection, some women asked if they could speak with me
without men present, and step by step, I began to meet with
women individually.[52] After six months, Medica invited me
to join its staff. I told them that a lot of bereaved women
needed encouragement to speak openly about their
experiences. This is how we began helping women who had
been raped and hadn't wanted to speak up before.

Many wanted to stay anonymous. I encouraged them to
tell their husbands what had happened. This was a huge
departure from our tradition, only possible after Racielema,
the chief officer in the Muslim community, passed a new
*fatwa*—a Muslim law—addressing the status of women who
had been raped. Before the fatwa, a lot of women felt sinful
because they had been raped. The chief officer explained that
their communities and family members should consider raped
women *shahid*, innocent people who had suffered atrocities.
That became the new religious law for these exceptional
times. Racielema asked men to help their wives and sisters,
stating that children born of rape are innocent. This fatwa was
important for women to accept their children and themselves,
and for men to bring forth understanding. Were it not for the
new fatwa, these women would have been in danger of being
expelled from their husband's homes and for bringing
dishonor upon their families.

At Medica, we introduced Aqiqah, a celebration for the
mother and the baby, where we welcomed the newborn and
accepted her or him as a new member of our community. We
did this for all the babies who came to their mothers by way
of rape. We said special prayers for the child, gave gifts, and
shared the satisfaction of motherhood with the mother. Aqiqah

---

[52] Not having men present in the group is very important for women who have
been raped. They have to feel completely safe even to begin talking about it.

helps women accept their children. It goes like this: "This is the child," I would tell the group. I'd then take the baby in my arms and say a prayer. When I was finished praying, I'd say, "This is the son of Sabiha. His name is Tarik. He is a member of our community. He is a beautiful gift from God." Then, when I was done, we passed the baby around and every woman gave the baby a blessing. Then we'd say another prayer. The mother was always the last to take the baby again. The idea was that after going around, the safest place to be is with your mother. Then the mother would speak, expressing very special feelings from her heart and soul for every child who was born, whether of rape or not. It was really helpful for these mothers to include this practice with every newborn. We wanted to integrate these children of rape with all the other children. Some women came because they were pregnant, and we included them too. We showed them that every child is a blessing, even when the birth is the result of rape. It was a ritual we made up out of necessity.

During the war, some of my clients stopped believing in God. One woman had been a believer, but when her son was killed in front of her house, she became angry with God. "If God is good," she told me, "if God is here to help me, why did He allow this to happen?" I understood her anger. It was part of the healing process, and it was important for me to support her. I told her it was okay to feel angry at her God, and I gave her an exercise to write what she wanted to say to Him. She wrote from her anger. After she was done, I asked her if she wanted to share it with me, burn it, or what? She decided to burn it, and she felt good afterward. But when she came back for our next session, she wondered what would happen if God got mad back. I told her it was okay, that God can't be angry at everyone He ever created. After that, she accepted her loss and tried to build a new relationship with her son and with God. For her, it was important to hear my opinion that God couldn't be angry at her. Some people are very strict about religion. It's hard for these kinds of people to help each other. When I work with clients like these who think God will punish them for everything, I say, "Then I don't want to believe. I don't want that kind of God."

Here at Medica we have a special room for prayer. For some women, their faith helps in their healing processes. During the war, Russians came to Bosnia and told us how they practiced Islam. They wanted us to practice the way they did. It's a problem when people impose their religion on you. My religion is my life. It helps me live more easily. When I speak with you, I am in my religion. I can't separate it from my life. Sometimes I work with husbands and wives around this aspect of religion. Often when a man becomes religious, he tells his wife she has to stay in the house and can't have contact with other men or wear makeup or dresses. If the wife wants to do any of these things, there's a conflict. When those men come here, we talk about it, and they are able to recognize that asking their wives to do these things makes their wives' lives more difficult. This helps the men and the women understand each other better. She tells him, "You can live in the way you want, but don't ask me to."

The word *forgiveness* was problematic during the war. Only when people realized that forgiveness meant helping yourself, not forgetting what happened, were they able to forgive. People sometimes think that if they forgive the person who killed their son, they also have to forget. Forgiveness is about leaving the negative energy behind and having space for positive energy. It's important to distinguish between forgiving and forgetting. When given a chance to think about this, the women realized they could forgive in order to open themselves to positive energy, but they didn't have to forget what happened to their family members. Because they didn't forget the person or the situation, they were in a better position to prevent further damage. Forgiveness helped them by completing their relationship with the person lost.

When I began this work, I started with the women who had been raped. After six months, I recognized it might be good to connect women from different therapy groups. I asked each of them if they'd like to work in gatherings of ten or fifteen. We could talk together and help each other recognize our strengths. It was important that they learn to help one another. In the healing process, religion, emotion, family, and economic situation are all important. Families either support a woman or make it difficult for her. Women needed to support women. They needed their strengths to be recognized again.

They began to work as one big group. After six months, I asked each of them to invite another woman to join the group. Then we worked with those women too. It was interesting to watch how they helped one another. Some newcomers were still in the same place emotionally as when they were raped. They hadn't talked about it until they were in the group. Then someone would say, "Aisha, your presence helped me when we were in Trebinje." In that way, we were building a self-help group. When someone asks how many women I helped at Medica, I cannot answer. I never really knew since I don't know how many of these women helped other women.

At the beginning, I needed to help myself. Then I realized that if I helped other people, I would be helping myself. Medica supported me with my own healing process. I started to regain trust in a better future. Seeing women of different backgrounds—Muslim (Bosniaks), Orthodox (Serbs), Catholic (Croats)—working together to help each other was paradise for me. It was hard work. I wondered how my Catholic friends were feeling, because in this town the majority is Muslim, and you never know what's happening on the street. But here we women stuck together, and I saw that people of all ethnic backgrounds wanted to help each other. It's actually our nature.

My desire to help people was fulfilled. My parents have returned to Vitez, and they have good relationships with their Croatian neighbors. Sometimes this creates problems with our Bosniak neighbors, but my parents don't mind. Wartime showed us that it's most important to be human. I don't pay attention to who practices which religion. I just look at people and find something good in everyone. God helped my family, and I remain open to Him. He helped me understand we would all return to Him. I believe that we're all here under observation, as though we're all taking a life exam, and we should work hard to pass it. People with genocide in their history need to help themselves first; then they need to assist other people. Peace is a lengthy process. Forgiveness is crucial. For some, it is nearly impossible, but forgiveness opens the door for our soul.

*"Every day, every hour [in the Nazi concentration camp], offered the opportunity to make a decision."*
— Viktor Frankl

Chapter 7
# Marijana Senjak
# Integrity

*"How did one preserve one's internal values
and also survive?"*

During the war in Bosnia, Marijana Senjak (Mar-ee-yán-a Sén-yak), a Croat clinical psychologist and single parent, made soul-searing choices about her daughter, Tamara. Becoming a single mother shortly after the war began, Mariana's relationship with her daughter is a central part of her story. A good mother nurtures and protects her child and is attuned to her needs. How Marijana nurtured her daughter during the war, and the complications war introduced into this effort, became part of her outlook on war in general.

Marijana likens Sabiha's and her work at Clinica Medica, and that of all peacebuilders, to a nurturing way of being, i.e., to "mothering," although that is not the word Marijana used. Marijana speaks eloquently on behalf of the feminine side of our natures—men's and women's—urging us to stop sending our boys to war, to stop destroying what we have built, and to start rebuilding our nest once and for all.

At Clinica Medica in Zenica, Marijana and her colleagues studied the writings of Victor Frankl, a Holocaust survivor and psychiatrist, and applied them to their work with rape victims. They asked Frankl's famous question, "Why didn't you kill yourself?" helping clients recognize why they chose to continue living, which in itself gave their lives meaning. During World War II, Frankl kept the image of his wife in his mind. Visualizing her from the men's side of the camp, hoping she was still alive on the women's side, Frankl felt that his wife expected him to suffer with dignity. Marijana believes that there is always someone who "expects us to suffer with dignity." The need to maintain dignity is essential to holding on to our humanity.

Although Marijana calls her options "luxury choices" compared to Frankl's, she still had to make choices about things most of us will never have to face. Her residual guilt as a Croat in Bosnia is a thread that runs throughout her interview, not because she would have harmed anyone, but because others of her nationality did. After the war, Marijana was nominated for a Nobel Peace Prize.

*Here is Marijana Senjak, in her own words:*
I was employed at Medica and also at the Iron and Steel Company in Zenica, Bosnia. In the summer of 1991 when the war started in Croatia, I was working in the Iron and Steel factory office when I got a call from my best friend, a colleague in Zagreb, Croatia. "It's coming," he told me. "War is about to break out in Bosnia. Prepare yourself. Make sure you have medicine and a survival kit for you and your baby."

I didn't believe war would ever break out in Bosnia. Back then Bosnia was part of Yugoslavia and even though war had broken out in Croatia, we in Bosnia were keeping community alive. "It's different here," I told him "We're keeping the community spirit of Yugoslavia alive." He said,

"There are already guns and grenades in Croatia." I am Croat and Catholic. I lived in Bosnia, had studied in Croatia, and I could not accept that it might happen here. I was hurt by what he said.

When war broke out in Sarajevo, it wasn't clear it was actually a war. It started as a workers' and artists' rally against the government to preserve peace in Yugoslavia. Bosnians were against the war, and our actions in the rally were genuine efforts for peace. But to my friend in Croatia, where war was already raging and Yugoslav soldiers were already committing atrocities, it looked as though we in Bosnia were trying to preserve something horrible that we thought was "peace." So we began to ask ourselves, "What *are* we preserving?" It wasn't clear.

The demonstration that triggered the war was nonviolent. Hundreds of Bosniak workers gathered to protest the Yugoslav government and ask for higher wages. That's when the first bullets were fired. Paramilitary, soldiers, snipers, and others began to act like terrorists, waiting in the Holiday Inn and the other buildings around the main square of Sarajevo to shoot the demonstrators. Suada Dilberović was the first victim. Her name is now on one of the walking bridges in Sarajevo. Another woman was also shot that day. Peace marches continued every day, along with killings, yet we found it impossible to believe that a war had started.

At the time, I was thirty. My daughter was fifteen months old. I'd been married for two years, but there were misunderstandings, and I knew our marriage wouldn't survive the war. Salaries had been lowered; everything was changing dramatically. Bosniaks are 99 percent of the population of Zenica. Before the war, you could greet others using Muslim, secular, or any greeting you wanted. We were multiethnic and proud of it. Now, suddenly, if you weren't Muslim, you couldn't use the traditional Muslim greeting *Salaam 'alaikum* ("Peace be unto you"). That was reserved for Muslims. *Dobar dan* ("Good day") became the socialist greeting, so when I went into a shop and said "Dobar dan," that signaled that I was either a Croat or a Serb, not a Muslim. Even though I was saying, "Good morning" or "Good afternoon," people wouldn't respond. Other changes were even more frightening. There were days I wasn't sure I'd have enough food for my baby or myself.

Serbian military from the former Yugoslav army were stationed on the eastern Bosnian border.[53] We called them weekend Chetniks, because they were ordinary people who mobilized on the weekends to fight and pillage in Bosnia. They stole from apartment buildings and sold their bounty on the black market in Montenegro and Serbia. Everyone stole, both material property and also positions and political or social advantage.

You had to hold on to your internal values, and at the same time you had to survive. How much could you do in the name of survival and still have self-respect? If someone offered you another's apartment, would you take it? If someone offered you a better job and it was someone else's, would you say yes? In Bosnia, it was both common and legal to enter someone's empty apartment and take their furniture. But it became a habit. A lot of people wanted to leave, but they couldn't sell their apartments because they belonged to the state. So they would say they were selling the furniture for very cheap. A person might give someone $500 for their furniture, and both parties understood that if you bought the furniture, you'd get the apartment too, because they were leaving. Sometimes soldiers just took over apartments. In those days, no one settled for an unfurnished apartment. When you took an apartment, you felt entitled to the furniture, too.

---

[53] Marijana sometimes called the former Yugoslavia "former Yugoslavia," because that's what it was when we were speaking, and she sometimes reverted to her old habit and called it "Yugoslavia." I leave it as she said it.

Legally, this was supposed to be okay. But when law is made according to personal interests and people are actually invited to behave in a way that isn't moral, you need to have the integrity to maintain your own value system. I have friends who wouldn't enter anybody's apartment. I wouldn't either. I lived in a very small apartment, and I still didn't take anybody else's. The difficulty came when you were in an extreme situation, your life was in danger, or you didn't have enough food for your child. We had to grapple with these dilemmas: Should I save my three-day food ration for my baby, or should I give some to other children who have even less? Every day during the war, we faced questions like that. Serb victims (as opposed to Serb perpetrators) often suffered the most. Other Serb victims as well as some of the women from Srebrenica whose family members had disappeared gathered and created community, making an effort to connect.

When danger is at its highest, some people develop a really strong solidarity with others. They help each other, sharing what they have. This is called the "honeymoon phase," one of shock and denial. After that phase, people organized to reach out more effectively. My colleagues and I were among the ones who organized. Some women, especially those with babies, felt their priority was to preserve the lives of their babies and themselves, so they weren't active in the community. My colleagues and I at Medica chose to be activists, but we never criticized those who made choices different from ours.

Eleven years later, we're still here. We see photos of our children at the beginning of the war and realize we weren't able to nurture them well. It was a matter of survival. I had to work twelve hours a day at a time my baby needed me physically and emotionally. I've done a lot of work around this in therapy. I had a lot of guilt until I was able to accept that I did what I had to do. It wasn't that I wanted to leave my baby alone, but I had to work to get money and food.

In Bosnia, especially in Zenica, there were six months when we were at the point of starvation. I was lucky to have a job. During a war, prices increase enormously. A bag of flour might cost $50 to $100. Women were selling their gold rings for 50 cents. My mother paid $5 for two eggs on the streets of Zenica. My friend sold a car for $125 to buy a bag of flour. We gave up everything that we earned and everything we owned to buy necessities. Food disappeared; grocery shelves were empty. There were no vegetables, just a few mushrooms, wooden-tasting onions, and a kind of wild grass we would never have eaten before the war. People collected these things in the forest and sold them. You had to go out early to collect them, sell them, or buy them. It was hard for most of us to think politically at first. I would tell people, "Don't tell me ideas! I don't want to analyze or even understand the political situation in the war." I was just angry and in survival mode.

Then in July 1992, seven colleagues and I organized, and Civil Defense gave us two offices in Zenica, where we founded the Center for Psychological Help in War. We invited teachers, psychologists, and psychiatrists from Zenica to join us. About twenty people supported us financially, and seven professionals actively helped us. The husband of one of my acquaintances was killed. Finally, it hit home that the war was really here.

Peace rallies continued. We joked about the old man on the eastern Bosnian border who blockaded the dam equipment on the mountain river of Drina, threatening to open the dam if they didn't stop the war. He was just one man, and in his mind, he could've created a huge lake! There were a lot of individual attempts like this to stop the war. We all had an impulse to do anything we could for the survival of the community. It was helpful but naïve. I collected my daughter's baby clothes and gave them to refugees who had babies. A lot of people did things like that. They also prepared food and brought it to the collection centers.

We started visiting refugee collection centers. Refugees came from central, eastern, and western Bosnia and settled in Zenica, because it was centrally located. No town was prepared for refugees, but every town provided all the facilities and personnel they had. Some refugees were put up in shop windows in the middle of town. Five hundred people stayed in unlit movie theaters. School sports arenas housed hundreds more. There was just enough room for them to sleep. They were given mattresses and they had plastic bags with all the belongings they could carry. The refugees kept their sense of humor about it all. They had lots of jokes and anecdotes about their plastic bags and what they'd brought with them.

Like them, I had a bag packed, including ironed cotton diapers, baby food, documents, jewelry, and my passport, and kept it with me all the time in case I had to flee. I still have it today. If war should break out again, I'm prepared to cross the border. Ever since 1992, I keep my basic documents with me.

I was especially impressed with the refugee center in the traditional town of Travnik. The center was a sports hall there, with 500 refugees in it. An American representative from UNHCR was sitting on a mattress with the refugees, fully engaged while she provided support. Nobody really knew how to act in these circumstances, so we had to learn from people like her. When the refugees invited us to sit down, we weren't sure how to respond. They'd offer us coffee, and we knew they couldn't afford coffee. So, we weren't sure whether to accept or not. They were already humiliated by their situation, so they watched us closely. Would we accept their invitation to sit on their mattresses? We learned: You sit on the mattresses and you accept the coffee. You sit and socialize. The next time we went, we brought our own coffee, sending a message that we are equals. In every situation, we gave them that message.

In the beginning, it was possible to give like this because we thought the war would last a very short time. No one thought it would last three or four years. In the later years of the war, refugees complained that Zenica wasn't providing as much help as they needed. Later we did research on the psychological consequences of the war. We talked to 200 refugees about how long they'd thought the war was going to last. Most had estimated about two months. That's what I thought, too. When it lasted longer, it became a question of surviving winters, then the spring. Then we were saying maybe it will be easier in the summer, always expecting it to be over soon.

It was difficult because we had an occupying army coming in and no weapons to defend ourselves. Both countries—Republika Srpska and Bosnia- Herzegovina—were under an arms embargo that had been imposed on us by the UNSC.[54] So, the Serbs were attacking us from the hills with weapons, and we couldn't defend ourselves.

I was one of the few people who spoke English, so I represented Medica at international feminist conferences to tell the delegates about the situation in Bosnia, particularly about war, rape, and the embargo.[55] Now everyone speaks

---

[54] In July 1991 the European Community and its member states decided to impose an arms embargo on the former Socialist Federal Republic of Yugoslavia. ... In September 1991, the United Nations Security Council decided to establish an arms embargo that applied to all of the territory of the former Yugoslavia in UNSC resolution 713. ("EU arms embargo on the former SFR of Yugoslavia—Bosnia and Herzegovina.) Stockholm International Peace Research Institute. November 12 2012.

[55] The use of rape in Bosnia was systematic and organized, designed to intimidate an entire population and to demoralize opposing troops. It began to be recognized as a war crime when eight Bosnian Serb military and police officials were indicted by the International Criminal Tribunal for the former Yugoslavia (ICTY) in June 1996. In 2001, three of them—Dragoljub Kunarac, Radomir Kovac, and Zoran Vukovic—were convicted for their involvement in the *Foča* rape camps. This outcome, with the ICTY recognizing rape as a crime against humanity, was a historic moment in international law. It was also of symbolic importance to the survivors. Their struggle

English, but in 1992, only a few of us did.[56] I learned a lot about peace and making connections in the midst of war. In Jerusalem, we received the Women in Black award for refusing violence, militarism, and war.[57] I went to Malta for the conference on Women Victims of War.[58] Representatives from Zagreb to Belgrade discussed the arms embargo in Bosnia. As peaceworkers and pacifists, they couldn't support the idea. TV cameras were there. There's a joke in Bosnia, "If Christiane Amanpour reports about you, something terrible is going to happen." We also joked about Bill Clinton lifting the embargo. In the Serbo-Croatian language, Bill means "will you?" Or "I will not be," or "I will not." So his name meant "maybe I will, maybe I won't." Would he lift the embargo? Bill.

Each time I traveled, people at home thought I wouldn't return. Sometimes my neighbors even told my daughter I wouldn't be back. But I always came back. One Bosniak official asked me, "Haven't you emigrated yet?" I was so surprised. I wasn't sure how to respond. Now I'm prepared for the question: Do you expect me to leave?

While I was traveling, I heard they were putting people into concentration camps back home. Again, it was hard to believe, because it wasn't happening to me. I needed time to

---

to heal emotionally and have their plight acknowledged was daunting. Peter Lippman, "Bosnia: Blood, Honey, and War's Legacy," www.opendemocracy.net/peter-lippman/bosnia-blood-honey-and-wars-legacy

[56] Jakob's prophecy about English becoming the lingua franca is coming true here. (See Chapter 7.)

[57] Women in Black is a worldwide network of women actively opposed to war, injustice, militarism, and other forms of violence. See womeninblack.org

[58] Association of Women Victims of War is a Sarajevo-based NGO that campaigns for the rights of women victims of rape and similar crimes committed during the Bosnian war. The association gathers evidence and information about war criminals and rapists hiding in the Republika Srpska to secure their prosecution. It provides key testimony in rape and sexual abuse trials linked to the conflict and helps obtain justice and financial and psychological assistance for many of its 1,000-plus members.

let in that this really was happening. It's hard to believe you are in danger when you aren't affected directly. You stay in denial. Until it's at your door or it's your child who gets killed, you don't believe it. But when it affects you directly, everything changes.

One day there was a shelling near my house. I lived near the Iron and Steel factory, where I worked. Refugees were settled in some of the offices. There was a sports hall near the administration building, where many more refugees were housed. The day of the shelling, we were working on an assessment with the refugees, and we heard screaming. A grenade had been thrown, but we didn't know where it landed. It sounded really close. Women at the refugee center began screaming, and we hid. After five minutes, we came out of hiding, went to the window, and saw refugees running. People were carrying big bags of flour out of the Iron and Steel factory. We didn't get paid in money, we got paid in food, and when the next grenade fell, flour dust and blood were everywhere. All the windows in the building were broken and pieces of grenade were everywhere. The walls had fallen out, and five people were killed right in front of us.

We went into my house. Earlier that day, my mother had picked up my daughter to take her to the park as she usually did, and now my daughter was sleeping on the small couch in the living room. One piece of grenade landed just short of her. Other pieces of grenade were in my closet; they'd just missed my clothes. I kept these pieces. A seven-year-old boy in my neighborhood was killed. My daughter was five. She used to play with him.

Until then, I had been active and stable, but for the next three months, I was in turmoil. I functioned but was constantly tense. The main question was whether we could survive if we stayed. Everyone had the right to leave. Many people left, but some of us stayed. Those who left just exchanged one set of problems for another. When I was in New York for a conference, I saw refugees from all over the world trying to survive—finding an apartment, a job, legal status, and so on. Though life was different there, it was as intense as here. In therapy, many couldn't focus on their trauma, because they were just trying to survive.

We who stayed in Bosnia learned that we could adapt to the situation here. Since we were here for four years, we didn't see differences in our country, but people who came back from Western countries saw differences. They complained that the administration was slow, the streets were dirty, the shop workers were unkind, and so on. They saw all these changes. Surviving, day by day, hour by hour, we had adapted.

I tried to help my neighbors, but since Croats were doing the shelling and I'm a Croat, it wasn't easy. I always feel guilty that Croats massacred others. During some of the shellings, a Bosniak neighbor invited my mother and daughter to come over to her side of the apartment building, where it was safer. We became close, but her husband still couldn't look at me because I'm a Croat. Then one Christmas, I saw him. He was Bosniak so he didn't celebrate Christmas, but he said Merry Christmas to me. Another Bosniak neighbor, his wife, was pregnant during one of the bombings. She fell down, and when the baby was born, his feet weren't in the proper position and he had to have surgery. Even though I'm a Croat, she and I became friends. I love her little boy and he loves me. He's joyful now, full of energy, really beautiful. I always said, "Good morning" and "Good evening," to everyone in my own language, and as I mentioned earlier, very few people would respond. Then one afternoon I went with another theologian to do outreach work in another city. Afterward, we went to the mosque to find the imam and his wife. An old man, who lived in the imam's apartment, was there in the mosque yard. This time when I said, "Good afternoon," he said, "Good afternoon" back. He belonged to the mosque, and yet he greeted me in the way that is appropriate for my religion. Those were moments of redemption.

I had similar experiences when we established the first therapy groups in Zenica in April 1993. A colleague from Croatia sent me a trauma handbook with lectures on the consequences of trauma and examples of interventions appropriate for groups that had been traumatized.

Nine groups of women survivors went through this process. Women's main fear back then was the topic of rape. Women who had been raped six to nine months earlier were really closed off from their feelings. So we didn't use the word *rape*. Our clients didn't either. They said "it" happened. We repeated "it" happened. We knew what "it" meant, but we never said rape. We weren't experienced, so everybody hesitated to approach the details. Women would tell us, "It happened to me in the concentration camps, but I don't want to talk about it in front of everyone. I will tell you in individual therapy."

Then a new woman came who had been raped just two days earlier and another arrived who had been raped just two weeks before coming in. They talked openly about what happened and encouraged us to talk too. I didn't know if I could stand it, if I could handle my own reactions without losing control. Every day we heard more than we'd heard before. I wrote a paper called "The Phenomenological Aspects of War Rape," giving a professional understanding of each aspect of rape. One aspect was the grotesque details of the violence, what I called "additional humiliation," but these were almost always stories of courage and humanity in extreme situations.

One client came to Medica asking how to tell her two school-age children that their father had been killed. He had been severely abused and tortured, even crucified and tied by a rope in his village. My client had seen his body. Her son was five, her daughter nine. She wanted to take them to a cafe and tell them in a nice environment to bring some beauty into it. It was so hard. I talked with my friend Edita about the grieving process. She had lost her husband and was left a widow with three children. Since she'd already been through the grieving process, I asked her how this woman might approach the situation.

While treating this woman, I learned that while her husband was being physically abused, she was imprisoned and being raped daily by a Serb commander. Whoever that commander wanted to rape, he just took outside and raped her. Some of the women were killed and then classified as missing. Men and women had been separated, and after she was raped, she was put back in with the women. Except, one time, the commander brought her into the room where the Bosniak men were kept and said to them, "Look at her. She is a whore. All of you, slap her face." It wasn't enough to rape her, he had to humiliate her even more in front of her own community. This is what I mean by *additional humiliation*.

One old man from the village said, "I know this woman, and I will not do it." What I learned from this story, and what I'm trying to communicate, is that it's hard to preserve your values in an extreme situation. We cannot expect everyone to behave like this old man. It happens perhaps once in 10,000 people. Not all of us are as strong as that. This man is a piece of gold. But he's proof that acting with integrity is possible. Atrocities and rape are on one side of the scale, and reactions like this man's are on the other. To me, his act balances the scale. Whenever I hear stories about trauma, I also hear stories about goodness. Even in the concentration camps, while some people were being heartless, others were helping. In Omarska camp, a Serb soldier, my client's son's classmate, surreptitiously provided the prisoners with glasses and food. I heard many stories of people on the perpetrator side who were secretly performing acts of kindness.

A Muslim woman from a village where 700 people had been killed and their houses burned by Croatians, joined our therapy group. She'd lost her husband, her thirteen-year-old son, two brothers-in-law, and her house. She had a fourteen-year-old daughter. Edita and I, who ran the group, are both Croats, and we felt a collective guilt. Five sessions passed. The woman kept repeating her traumatic story. It took twenty minutes each time. She stopped when she got to the point where her son was trying to tie his sneakers and a sniper shot him. We didn't know a lot about trauma theory, so we just reacted how we felt. The sixth time, she said to me, "Marijana, you are Croat, but you didn't make this situation." Some of the most vulnerable clients were able to accept people from other ethnic backgrounds without accusing anyone. They didn't think about who was guilty in terms of politics or ethnicity or religion. They could distinguish between perpetrators and those who had nothing to do with their trauma. This woman was letting me know we weren't responsible for her tragedy, and it gave me the courage to stay here, to help people who needed it, and not to worry about my own background. She released me from guilt by association.

Later we learned that when a client repeats a story over and over, the emotional content has not yet been touched. This woman went on to do really well. She came to Medica for a while, because she couldn't go home. Then she became a witness at The Hague, and this activism provided a lot of internal satisfaction. She's a strong, determined, practical woman—the sort of person who wants to take action. I love that.

Eventually, we discovered the importance of staying emotionally connected to the story. In the beginning, we didn't even know the word *trauma*. We used the word *injury*.[59]

---

[59] Today some clinicians use the term *moral injury* to describe the kind of trauma that is experienced by both victims and perpetrators of war. See Rita

We created our own approach by collecting information, trying different things, and seeing what worked. I usually work with the body, using imagery or something like that to relax the body. At first, our not being trained put us at a disadvantage. Our clients were traumatized, and so were we. Because of the continued shelling, it was very intense.

Then *The Courage to Heal* by Ellen Bass was published, and we pored over the book, dedicating two sessions to each stage she proposes.[60] Ellen Bass explains that forgiving the perpetrator is not crucial to recovery, but it's crucial to forgive yourself and find spiritual meaning in your life. In 1997, Judith Herman's *Trauma and Recovery* was translated in the Bosnian cities of Tuzla and Sarajevo and published here.[61] Judith Herman says you can't be the same after trauma, but that in recovery you develop characteristics you could not have had before. You grow and acquire new skills and a new understanding of life and society. Her perspective helped me lower my expectations. Now I'm satisfied with small changes. If women have more energy, become more active, have a new hairstyle, wear different colors, or make one small step forward, it makes me happy.

A fifteen-year-old girl from eastern Bosnia who had been raped came to Medica. Her father and brother were still missing, and she had escaped with her mother. She doubted she could finish high school because so many years had passed since she'd been in school. Eventually she did, completing courses in reading, dancing, English, computer,

---

Nakashima Brock and Gabriella Lettini, *Soul Repair: Recovering from Moral Injury after War* (Boston: Beacon Press, 2012). See also Edward Tick, PhD, *War and the Soul: Healing Our Nation's Veterans from Post-traumatic Stress Disorde.* (Wheaton, Illinois: Quest Books, 2005).

[60] Ellen Bass and Laura Davis, *The Courage to Heal: A Guide for Women Survivors of Child Sexual Abuse* (New York: Harper Collins, 1988).

[61] Judith Herman, *Trauma and Recovery: The Aftermath of Violence—from Domestic Abuse to Political Terror* (New York: Basic Books, 1997).

and cooking. When you look at what she achieved even with her trauma, it's remarkable.

Gabriella, our therapist and teacher, taught us to use psychodrama to heal trauma. In one exercise, you take a pile of gem stones and ask women to choose a few that they like and have them represent their inner strengths, internal beliefs, and people they can rely on. Then they use the gems to present themselves to the group. They might say, "This fine, strong stone is my husband. He is like a rock. He is always there for me." Recognizing the strengths they have, they work through their trauma using the jewels. Holding something beautiful, they are able to talk about things that are hard. They link beauty with trauma, by bringing beauty into it, which is what we wanted them to do.

Women who have been through the most difficult trauma, especially Srebrenica women, might not be able to use the gems as symbols of strength, but they can still use them to tell their stories. Choosing a black one, they might say, "It was July when my husband disappeared. And this green one is my hope he will return. And these three are my children." Preoccupied by their trauma, they need longer to reconnect with their strengths. Afterward, we might have them set the stone down and put a circle around it. Then they just color and write things like "strength, hope, my husband."

We also do "the river of life" exercise, where we take out a big piece of paper and draw a river through the middle of it. We divide the paper into four parts: past, war, present, future. We tell the women, "This is the river of life. It connects the pieces of our life. Draw each chapter along banks of your life." When they finish, we ask them to present what they have drawn. Again, this exercise aims to combine beauty with trauma. We are trying to reintegrate the traumatized client's experience. The black box that represents war is not a border that splits this life from the one before. It's one episode in a woman's life. We tell them it was four difficult years, not your whole life.

Another powerful exercise is called "last meeting with a person." We ask the women to close their eyes, and then we say, "Imagine an important person in your life. Think about the last time you saw him or her. Remember what you wanted to tell them, or what they told you. Now, open your eyes and draw a picture of this last encounter." This is a really important exercise, especially for the Srebrenicans. As a group, the Srebrenicans lost 8,000 people. One old Srebrenican woman lost twenty-eight members of her family. On average, each Srebrenican is missing eight people.

Nurka, a therapist friend of mine, was working with a Srebrenican woman who showed no visible signs of recovery. The woman was focusing on the last time she saw her husband. He left the house and disappeared. Nurka asked her, "What were the last words he said to you?" The woman said, "He told me to take care of myself and the children." Nurka works quite directly. Sometimes she jokes about her interventions and calls them "crazy interventions." So she asked again, "What were his last words?" The woman repeated it. Nurka asked her again, "*Who* did he tell you to take care of?" She made her repeat it and repeat it. She kept saying, "*Who* did he tell you to take care of?" The woman finally got it. "He told me to take care of *myself.*" It was really hard for her to let it in. These exercises might sound easy, but they address monumental losses.

We also cut out paper hearts and gave them to the women to make them as beautiful as they wanted, to put whatever and whoever was in their heart onto the paper—all the people they loved, the things they enjoyed, everything! "Even the ones who died or disappeared?" they'd ask. "If they are in your heart, then yes, put them on the paper." They did all sorts of things, not always intense, sometimes just funny. One of the young women drew blue jeans in her heart, along with yogurt and fruit. She made it into a sign for her door. "If you need two sides," we told her, "use both sides. Include whatever is in your heart."

In English, you say, "healing from trauma." Here in Bosnia, we reserve the word healing for medicine. In our language, healing is close to the word *cure*, to make well. When we use the word *healing*, it means we've really cured somebody. We're not approaching this work with the assumption that we can *cure* anyone. It's not possible. The consequences of this war will last for half a century. So we can't say someone is "healed." We can't even say someone has recovered. We only hope they accept their losses and pick up their lives. Their lives will never be the same as before. They aren't healed. So we use the word *recovery*.

I've grown a lot spiritually. Like many people from socialist countries, I thought of myself as an atheist. I wasn't a hard communist, but I had read Marx, and I agreed with what he said. He said the happiest people in the world are those who help the most people. I still believe in the humanistic values behind the communist approach, but when it becomes an ideology, socialism does not always know how to take care of people's needs.

I was educated in humanistic psychology, which was the groundwork for my career. At the beginning of the war, my faith was based on trusting human beings, a belief that human nature is fundamentally good. The war put these basic beliefs into question. I used to think if you do good things, good things will happen to you. If you are careful with people and do as much good as you can, no bad will come to you. Even if people aren't grateful, good will come back to you somehow. I spoke about this with Edita, and she said that everything that happened needed to happen. Spiritually, we don't know why it was needed. I would joke with her, "Okay, it was needed, but in such proportion?"

During the war, I began to understand God. In dangerous situations, everyone relies on the spiritual. I asked

God for help. It was like a dream, but really intense, as though real. I remember the feeling. When my clients thanked me, I would tell them, "Don't thank me; thank God." I didn't ask for anything in return. I only prayed that God would give me good health so I could keep helping people and provide for myself and my daughter.

My daughter has her own interest in religion. My ex-husband is an Orthodox Christian Serb, and I am Catholic Croat. In the 1990 census, we declared ourselves "Yugoslavs," neither Orthodox nor Catholic. We decided not to baptize our daughter. My daughter asked me, "Who should I love most—my mother, my father, or God?" I told her I wasn't sure and would ask Sabiha, since she's a theologian. Sabiha said, "God. Then through God, you can love your mother and father."

Even though I don't go to church, I'm now a believer. I learned God again. In the evenings when I'm done with work, I read poetry. Sometimes I read haiku poetry. I really like Borges. I read from the Koran and from the Bible. They're almost the same. If I have questions, I read a few pages until I find the answer. I find a passage that is parallel with my situation, and I ask myself, "What does this tell me? What is the message?" I find solutions in the Koran and the Bible.

Our approach to the media, to sharing our stories with the world, is to tell the truth. Our clients say it simply, "I want the truth to be told." The truth about Bosnia. It was never clear to the outside world what sort of war was going on here. It's really important that the truth be told, especially the stories about war rape. We want people to know about the center's work. We have nine departments and fifty-nine employees. It's impossible to fund it from Bosnia alone. We need support. So, we want journalists to help spread the word, to present our work and pass it around the world.

# The Sarajevans
# Jakob Finci, Salih Rasavać, and Vjekoslav Saje

Jakob Finci, Salih Rasavać, and Vjekoslav Saje were presenters at the Karuna Center for Peacebuilding and Conflict Transformation seminar in Sarajevo in March of 2003. Each of their presentations was so riveting that I asked if they would consent to being interviewed for this book the following spring. They all agreed. By the end of the interviews, all three had shared the workings of their minds and hearts during the genocide, especially as it played out in the siege of Sarajevo, where they lived. Sarajevo was the "belly of the beast," the epicenter during the war. Since each is a prominent community leader, their stories shed light on the nature of leadership in a crisis like this. It involves creativity, duty, optimism, and moral courage.

*"Studies of rescuers of Jews during World War II ... have shown that empathy played a major role in their helping behavior. ... This required the very highest levels of inner strength, courage, and moral integrity—and it was often the power of empathy (and of course compassion ...) that helped them mobilize these heroic qualities."*
— The Dalai Lama

# Chapter 8
# Jakob Finci
# Duty

*"It was my duty"*

Jakob Finci (Yáh-kobe Fín-chi), a leader in the Jewish community in Sarajevo, played a key role for elders of all ethnicities during the siege of Sarajevo. His was the best, cleanest, most well-appointed office I visited in Sarajevo. A beautiful, dark, cherrywood table lay glistening in the middle of it, and a secretary outside took calls for him as needed. The phone rang frequently; he's clearly an important man. The feeling of pressure in the room was palpable, making my time with Jakob different from the other interviews.

Jakob spoke fast, in excellent English. Of all of my Bosnian narrators, Jakob Finci most demonstrated the importance of heritage, which in his case was Jewish as well as Yugoslavian. Acting in the true spirit of brotherhood and unity that had united the former Yugoslavia, Mr. Finci took courageous action. At the end of the interview when asked what led him to do the work he did during the war, Jakob replied, "It was my duty." When everything is in chaos and what to do next is by no means clear, this knowledge can show the next step. Duty, for Jakob, was not a joyless center-post. He always made sure his work included celebration.

By the end of our interview, I felt a palpable force emerging from Jakob Finci. Like all of my informants, Jakob was holding a lit candle in the midst of great darkness, blessing and binding the wounds of his countrymen and women.

*Here is Jakob Finci, in his own words:*
I was the first member in my family in three-and-a-half centuries to be born outside of Sarajevo. In 1943, the year I was born, my family was detained in an Italian camp for Jews on the Croatian island of Rab. We survived because the Italian camps were less harsh than the camps in Germany or the ones held by the Ustasha.[62] After the war, my family came back to Sarajevo, partly out of nostalgia, a "typical Jewish disease," but really, America was far away and closed, and Europe was destroyed, so the best we could do was to come back home.

I grew up in Sarajevo and finished my schooling here, including the university, where I was trained as a lawyer, specializing in commercial law and international arbitration. Before the war here, I worked in a large Yugoslav sporting company, exporting sports equipment worldwide. We had more than fifty factories in Yugoslavia, with more than 50,000 employees.

In November 1990, we had our first post-World War II democratic elections. Three national parties defeated the

---

[62] Ustasha was the ultranationalist fascist group that controlled Croatia during World War II, even more brutal than their Nazi counterparts. www.ground-report.com/croatians-react-to-concentration-camp-commanders-death

socialist communist party.[63] Soviet Communism was "red"; our socialism was "pink." It was communist socialism, not as tough as in some other Eastern European countries. We are considered Western to them, even though the West considers us Eastern. Before this election, we had been allowed to have student associations, workers associations, human organizations, but not Jewish, Muslim, or Croat organizations. We couldn't have any national organizations, but after the 1990 elections, the new government let us form national societies again.

So, in February 1991, we started La Benevolencia again, a Jewish cultural, humanitarian, and educational society first established in Bosnia in 1892. Before the Holocaust, it was the umbrella organization for almost all Jewish activities. We tried to showcase the richness of Jewish culture that we had brought to Bosnia 500 years ago. And side by side with these cultural activities, we did humanitarian work.

In the middle of 1991, war broke out in Slovenia and Croatia. Dubrovnik, a small Croatian town with a tiny Jewish community of about thirty people, was under siege for ninety-one days. Of course, ninety-one days is nothing compared to the 1,400 days Sarajevo was under siege, but Dubrovnik was a good lesson for us. The average age of Jews there was between seventy-five and eighty, and these elders needed medicine. Bosnia is located between Croatia and Serbia, and is practically a tax-free zone, so we transferred medicine and other assistance to our friends in Dubrovnik and learned the importance of having enough medicine here in case something happened. It showed us how to prepare, even though President Izbegović kept saying, "Don't worry, there will not be a war in Bosnia. We have been together for so long,"[64] and

[63] Viktor Meier, *Yugoslavia: A History of its Demise*, Trans. Sabrina Ramet (New York: Routledge, 1999), 193.
[64] Alija Izetbegović became the first president of the newly independent Republic of Bosnia and Herzegovina in 1992.

so on. Using our Jewish instincts, a kind of genetic knowledge, we began to prepare. We sensed that a war was coming.

First we met with the doctors and pharmacists of the Jewish community and asked them to prepare lists of what would be needed for our elders. La Benevolencia had 1,200 members at the time, half over 55. Then we asked friends and donors abroad to send medicine. Second, we stockpiled food. We bought porridge, oil, sugar, and flour, just in case. We thought that if everything turned out okay, we could distribute these things to people in need. Third, we asked all the members of the community to renew their passports in case of evacuation. Yugoslavia didn't have diplomatic relations with Israel; they were cut off in 1967. With passports, we could travel almost anywhere except Israel. For Israel and Russia, we needed a special exit visa. So we had people renew their passports and obtain an Israeli exit visa, just in case. Thirty to fifty people in our Jewish community traveled to Israel annually to visit family. Suddenly 400 of us were asking for exit visas to Israel. The daily newspaper, *Oslobodjenje*, ran an article that said, "When Jews flee a city, don't go there."

The war in Bosnia started in Sarajevo on April 6, 1992, with demonstrations, barricades, and sniper fire. A lot of elders said, "I survived World War II. I'm too old to go through this again. Please help me get out of Bosnia." So on the tenth of April, just four days after the start of the war, we organized the first evacuation. The Belgrade Airport was still open. The elders flew from Sarajevo to Belgrade and then to different countries from there.

The second exodus was on the April 17, eleven days later. People had started to say, "I wasn't aware it would be so dangerous. I wasn't ready to leave, but I am now. The third evacuation was on May 1. We had three huge airlifts. The elders and most of our children went abroad. We had to split families. Almost all the children went to Israel. Some of the elders moved to Jewish old-age homes in Switzerland and an old-age home in Zagreb, the only one in the former Yugoslavia (now in Croatia). Some stayed in Belgrade because they didn't think the war would last all that long. The war in Croatia had only lasted a few months, and the one in Slovenia only seven days. We had also been witness to wars in the Middle East, but they lasted only a few days.

On May 2, the siege of Sarajevo started. That's when the real hell began. Sarajevo was looted from the inside. Every shop—except the bookshops—was looted. No one was interested in books until September, when they realized books could be burned for fuel. At that point, the bookstores and the pharmacies were looted. So we opened a pharmacy for our community and started distributing medicine for free. We had stockpiled enough for 500 elders, and since only 100 Jewish elders were still in Sarajevo, we had five times more medicine than we needed. So we shared it on a humanitarian basis, asking only, "What do you really need?" Thousands of people took advantage of this, and La Benevolencia supplied 40 percent of the medical needs of the citizens of Sarajevo. The humanitarian community, people from abroad, including pharmaceutical companies and huge NGOs, sent surplus medications that were near their expiration dates. The World Health Organization (WHO) was useless. It sent a lot of antimalarics because 400 years ago malaria was a problem here. WHO also sent water. At that time, the only thing we had in Sarajevo was water, but WHO sent water because it was on some list it had.

During that time, Sarajevo was cut off from all sources of electricity, gas, and telephone service. We were basically a huge camp. We had reserves of beans, pasta, and rice, but you can't eat these without cooking, and how could we cook if there was no energy? So we opened a soup kitchen using a woodstove, and cooked using two huge, twelve-gallon pots, enough for 350 hot meals. We also burned some coal that we had in our basement for the central heating of our community. We were able to help others on a nonsectarian basis.

Almost all the Jews in Sarajevo are descendants of Jews who arrived here from Spain beginning in 1565. The Ottoman Empire had just conquered Bosnia, and they accepted Jews with open arms. The first synagogue in Sarajevo was built in 1581. That's how long there has been a Jewish presence in Bosnia, especially in Sarajevo. Jews lived mostly in cities and towns and worked in the professions. Compared with the treatment of Jews in the rest of Europe, it was much better here. There was no ghetto, no special rules. Jews were treated like all the other non-Muslims.

Sarajevo's Jewish quarter is on the west side of the river. The man who owned the shop in front of the Jewish community was Muslim. We'd been friends for a long time. He had to close his business during the war, so he invited us to use his shop as our pharmacy. So during the war, we had a real pharmacy in a real shop. For the Bosnians it was not easy to pronounce La Benevolencia. The consonants are too soft. It's an old Spanish term meaning "good will." The military called it the "Jewish Pharmacy." After the siege began, it was clear that if you needed something, you could go to the Jewish Pharmacy. If you couldn't find it there, you had to give up because it just didn't exist. To reach our pharmacy, you had to cross the bridges, which was always dangerous. So people asked us to open a second pharmacy in another part of town, which we did, in front of the national theater. We called it the City Pharmacy. It's still in the same location. You could get medicines without crossing the bridges.

We were distributing food and medicine, and we began to wonder what else we could do. At first, we offered classes in foreign languages: English, French, German, Hebrew, and Arabic. The best professor of Arabic was Jewish. We told people that English was becoming the lingua franca, and whether you were an optimist or not, it was better to learn English than anything else. It was a practical suggestion, suggesting that our world might be taken over by English-speaking people, so you'd better learn English.

September 1992, five months after the war started, was the commemoration of 500 years since the expulsion of Jews from Spain. We organized a huge cultural event called *Sepherat* 92. Sepherat is the old Ladino word meaning "west of Spain." Sepherat 92 was the first cultural event held in Sarajevo during the war. We had exhibitions, concerts, roundtables, and lectures at the Holiday Inn. The hotel was made of concrete, so it was safe. All the journalists covering the war were staying in the hotel, so news about Sepherat 92 was on the front page of the *New York Times*. It was really incredible to have a cultural event in the middle of a war. All of Sarajevo attended—the president, members of the government, everyone. Among those who came was a Palestinian doctor who had trained in Sarajevo, gotten married, and stayed. He ran a small hospital in Dobinga, near the airport, far from the city center. At Sepherat 92, he approached me and said, "I'm a Palestinian, you are Jews, so we're almost cousins. People from Dobinga cannot reach your pharmacies. Can you put a pharmacy in my hospital?" Naturally we said yes. So the third Jewish pharmacy opened, run by a Palestinian doctor. It was successful and proved that anything is possible with a little good will, *la benevolencia.*

Sarajevo was divided in half at the time. The western side of the river was under Serbian control, completely cut off from the rest of the town. Life was quite different from before. La Benevolencia kept distributing medicines and food, and we kept evacuating elders out of the city. It was clear not everyone was going to survive here, so we tried to help people leave. To do that, we had to prepare a lot of paperwork. We organized eleven evacuations during the war, helping 1,000 Jews and 1,500 others leave. I think we were able to get people out because we were helping everyone on a humanitarian basis, so people helped us in return. Perhaps they thought the Jews had paid the price in the last war, so why not help them get out this time. Another reason might have been that all three sides were afraid of international public opinion. I was speaking with a *New York Times* correspondent, and he explained that his readers couldn't see the difference between Serbs and Croats, but if three Jews were killed by Serbs or five by Croats, that was news. That's my theory of how we were able to succeed. At the same time, we've always been in good relations with all three groups, and using these connections, we were able to organize. I did it because it was my duty.

*"Trauma is bigger than expertise of any sort—it's in our midst, in our language, our wars, even the ways we try to love, repeating, repeating."*
— Annie Rogers

# Chapter 9
# Salih Rasavać
# Optimism

*"What kept me going is that I'm an optimist.*
*... I was sure I would survive."*[65]

The office of Salih Rasavać (Sá-lee Rá-sa-vach) is in a high-rise apartment building near Sarajevo's well-known Holiday Inn, in an area that became known during the war as Sniper Alley. The Holiday Inn was only partially restored after the war; it was still riddled with bullet holes when I was last there in 2010, an eerie reminder of the evil acts committed there. Five flights of concrete stairs lead to Salih's darkened office.

---

[65] Optimism is another of the traits identified by Seligman and Peterson as transcendent. They write: "Hope and optimism are incompatible with anxiety or depression. They energize us. They direct us. They give us something to which to look forward." Christopher Peterson and Martin Seligman, *Character Strengths and Virtues: A Handbook and Classification* (Oxford University Press, 2004), 526-527.

Salih is a balding, former folk dancer, now a social worker. Grace radiates in his fanciful, sweeping gestures. Highly expressive, Salih is a model of emotional honesty. "How can we make it through anything, if we are not honest about our lives?" he asks. There is a fluid quality to his sweetness, his humility, and his courage. Tears flowed freely, quickly followed by thoughtful reflection, then anger, and finally, gratitude, when he spoke of his son during our first interviews in 2004. By 2010, when I did the final interviews, Salih no longer expressed any sadness about his son and was full of joy about his new granddaughter.

Salih does not think of himself as courageous, though others certainly see him that way. He believes that people are courageous only if they overcome fear and since he was never afraid, he doesn't believe he was courageous. Something in him just acted, and it took the form of valorous, rescuing actions. That something, he believes, is *optimism*. While a pessimist might despair and think there's no point, an optimist feels impelled to take action to help. Optimism keeps one expecting good, even in the midst of evil. Salih did not despair. He got angry and he took action, over and over again. Optimism informed his decisions and sustained him.

*Here is Salih Rasavać, in his own words:*
I was born and grew up in Sarajevo. I completed my studies in social work, was married, and raised a son and two daughters here. Before the war, I worked as a social worker with young people who had drug and alcohol problems. When the war started, like all parents, I was frightened and confused. It was extremely dangerous, and I needed time to understand what was happening. I was wondering what to do for our children. I lost almost 50 pounds in three months, not because we didn't have food—we had food—but because it was so stressful and confusing for me.

When the war started, a woman came to Sarajevo and organized an educational training focusing on trauma, PTSD, psychosocial interventions, and therapy. I told her about our life before the war, explaining that my daughter used to like good perfume. I'd been a choreographer and a dancer in a well-known Arab folk dance group. When I traveled, which I did a lot, I would bring her back hair perfume. The woman tried to give me half a bottle of perfume. I told her, "I don't want you to give me anything. I only want to explain to you what conditions were like for my family before the war. *We all have prewar identities and ways of living. War changes all that.*"

Just before war broke out, when snipers began surrounding the city, the young people in our neighborhood organized themselves to protect us. My son was one of them; he was sixteen. It's hard to explain what it felt like to see my own teenage son with a gun. My son's best friend's father held a high position in Belgrade. I met the boy's mother and told her I wanted to send my son away. Sarajevo was closed; only Serbs could leave the country. The next morning, I think it was April 20, her husband sent a small plane and I was able to send my son with their family to Serbia. He was in Belgrade for about three months. After that, I sent him to live with cousins in Sweden, and he spent the whole period of the war there. Now he's finishing his studies in Spain. My youngest daughter was in medical school here in Sarajevo and spent the war with us. My other daughter spent three months in London working for the Associated Press. A colleague of hers was killed there. The UN High Commissioner for Refugees (UNHCR) transported them both to the hospital in London. Then she came home.

I feel as if I lost my son during this period, even though I was trying to save him. He was sixteen when he went away. When he came back, he was angry, afraid what people would say about him. Before the war, we had a close relationship. The whole war he had to be away from his family. When he first got home, he spent ten days in his room and would only talk to his older sister. He wouldn't speak with his mother, me, or his younger sister. He still lives abroad in Spain and visits us for a week or two every year. I feel like I lost a child, and it makes me sad. Later I will give an example of the judgment that people who kept their children passed on us who sent ours away. My son was afraid of being judged. The issue of what to do with our most vulnerable family members, especially children and elders, was central for us during the war.

During the war, I worked in Markale selling books and pictures for food. Grenades fell every day, and I survived. Others took the hit instead of me. I'm not religious, so it wasn't religion that kept me going, although religion helped a lot of my clients. What kept me going was optimism. I believe in people. I saw people in need, and I asked the city government to designate a building for the refugees from many places on the street. They gave me the key to a school sports facility. Some colleagues and I organized and began doing humanitarian work. That helped me. I was less concerned about myself while I was taking care of others. It gave my life meaning and purpose.

For six months, I worked at the International Rescue Committee. We were basically in the same position as the people we were helping, but we kept on working. We had to do *something*, even if it was just to go out and try to find water. Sometimes I felt like I was working without a reason, but I never felt tired. It's difficult to explain. I was always ready for action. Everyone asked where I got my strength, and I told them, "I'm no stronger than you are, but I push myself into action." Part of the reason I could do it was that my emotional reaction was not there. When the war started, I was emotional, but when I started mobilizing, I was devoid of emotion.

If I saw a wounded child or someone on the street, I was always the first to help, and I did it without feeling. I'd find assistance, I'd get them a car, but I didn't feel anything. When the situation is that dire, instinct just kicks in. When my daughter was wounded in Sarajevo, I took her to the hospital without emotion. But when UNHCR sent her to London to work for the Associated Press, I cried for a week. When you're fighting for survival, you don't have time for emotions.[66] They get in your way. You just have to act. If you try to take care of yourself emotionally, you lose the time and energy you need to survive. When I was alone, I would ask myself, "Am I normal? What's happening to me? Why am I like this?" You help, but at the same time, you feel nothing. Was it a kind of psychosis?

During the war, many of my clients' emotions were blocked like mine. Now that the war is over, it's time for us to feel our emotions. People think now that we have peace in Bosnia-Herzegovina, we don't need support from psycho-social services, but we need them more than ever. I'm working as a volunteer in Srebrenica with Corridor, an association of mental health practitioners that provides services on a humanitarian basis.

I met a woman named Katim, about seventy-six years old. When I saw her in Srebrenica, she was really happy. "Oh Salih, you have to visit me in my home and have a cup of coffee." In the yard in front of her house was a grave. I asked if we were alone in her house, and she said yes. I asked why she had returned; she said she had to. Then she showed me her son's grave. She knows who killed him because they were holding her and made her watch while the man did it. Her neighbors forced her to dig up the grave and bury him again properly. She said, "I have to care for the grave, put flowers near it, make sure it's clean." I asked if she would stay in Srebrenica, and she said, "Yes, I will." When I asked why, she said, "Revenge." Her being there was a punishment to the

---

[66] I learned a great deal from Salih about this, and I believe he is exactly right. The "conscious suffering" comes later, not during a crisis. During a crisis, to "make it through," we must cling to our centerposts and not deviate from our goals. Later, we can feel again. We see this with all the interviewees to one degree or another.

man who did it. "When he sees me on the street, he knows I know. It's a message, reminding him of what he did." She told me the first time she saw him on the street, she saw fear in his eyes. That's enough for her. She knows that whenever he sees her, he is in fear. I ask myself, "What would I do if I were in her position?"

It is complex to be an advisor in Srebrenica because we're in transition on all levels. All over Bosnia, the family is in transition. When I work, I always ask about the family. Most families lost one or more members. Now we have a new model of the family. One of my clients lost her son in the war. He was my son's age. During one session, she told me, "I don't like people who sent their sons somewhere else during the war. My son was killed here. If I were in a position of power, I would put all the people who sent their sons out of Sarajevo into that permanent fire on Central Street, so everyone can come spit on them."

I was traumatized by what she said and told my supervisor I couldn't continue to work with her. Luckily, we get together and process the work we do with clients. One of the psychologists from my staff told me she sometimes feels like a garbage can. Though we are prepared to take in this garbage and listen to these issues, we also have our own issues. My colleagues told me, "Salih, don't stop. You can do it," so I continued. At the end of one of my sessions with this client, I told her about my son and explained my feeling toward her when she told me what she had. She took my hand. "Don't be angry with me. Yours was the right choice. You helped me understand myself. Now I know I was jealous. It hurt me that my son had to stay." Today she is very active in a parents' organization and a representative in Parliament. And we're really close.

In school, we didn't learn enough about trauma. Now I sometimes wonder if my wartime activity had to do with my own childhood trauma. My mother died when I was a teenager, and I was raised by other family members. During the war, I was never afraid for myself. I never ran. When I was on Central Street, or Sniper Street, where they had us in the palms of their hands if they wanted to shoot us, I never ran and I wasn't afraid. I was sure I would survive. I worked with a lot of children who lost their parents during the war. We made a movie about it. That work has been part of my own healing. Perhaps sending my son away was part of it too.

The best way to help yourself is to talk about your experiences during the war. Psychosocial work focuses on helping individual clients, but our interventions have to work toward healing society, too. We support our clients in order to effect changes in society, because it's society that produces the conditions that lead to war. We have to think about the future. Most professionals are ready to speak with clients about their immediate trauma. A woman is raped and she tells you a story about it. We talk about the actual rape, while forgetting that she is also a refugee. She lost her husband, her house, her past. We need to include the whole field, not just one event as if it's isolated. When we speak about trauma in a place like Srebrenica, we are speaking about a series of events, and we have to take into account the whole social structure that has been changed. We have to look at trauma in Bosnia as a whole and teach our clients about politics and context. We have to be more active before elections. Part of healing our clients involves getting them to become active in order to heal society as a whole.

Most of the people I work with are healing from war trauma. From time to time, people ask me, "Salih, when will it end?" There is no end. In the future, professionals will be working on intergenerational trauma. Unhealed trauma passes from one generation to the next. During the war, young people's only care was to enjoy life. Now, after the war, especially in Bosnia, Croatia, and Serbia, we have problems with drugs, especially among the children of those who haven't gotten help sorting out their feelings. We have to find our own model.

145

I went to a daylong workshop on conflict resolution in Srebrenica, but it was too short. We need to be learning about tolerance and teaching about collective problems, including how to deal with returnees. We need to find out if they need assistance. When people start to speak, we can open the door—very slowly—into the problem. Serbs were traumatized, too, but their war trauma was less. They compare their trauma with that of the other groups, but it's not the same. They do it for political gain and take it all the way to The Hague to lessen the charges against them. Perpetrators need psychotherapy the most. Even though they were sometimes victims themselves, for the most part, they were complicit with evil. For perpetrators to heal, they need to *feel* what they've done, not deny it. But it isn't happening here. Justice is not served by inattention to perpetrators' real needs.

Near Sarajevo, nearly 150 women were raped in one small village. The judges at The Hague just sent the women to other countries, to Germany, for example, but the German government wouldn't give them papers to stay. They sent them back to Bosnia. Now, they're at "transition centers" in Bosnia while their houses are being rebuilt. It's traumatic for them to return home. I'm working with a family from Bjeden. For six months a neighbor raped the woman. Finally the International Red Cross arrived. They sent her to Vienna, then brought her back. She's waiting for her house to be rebuilt too. The neighbor who raped her is free, and she's afraid to press charges because he's still in the community. She feels suicidal but doesn't want to kill herself because she has two children. We see this over and over among those waiting to return to their homes.

Last month I spent a week at The Hague. Some cases from The Hague will be taken over by local courts here in Sarajevo. They called in professionals and taught us how to be witnesses when the cases are brought to our local courts. I was present at The Hague when Milošević was at the court, and the commander who perpetrated the siege of Sarajevo was on trial. The commander got twenty years. I was devastated. Twenty years is not enough for someone who destroyed so much. The problem with these trials is that there isn't enough evidence. Even though everybody knows that Sarajevo was under siege, they don't have sufficient proof of specific crimes.

People see themselves as victims and then do nothing. Passivity keeps them in a victim role. They want to return to the past they had before the war; they don't want to go forward. The first time I went to a village where many people were killed, I saw one old house with a few middle-aged people drinking coffee. I asked if I could join them. "Where are you from?" they asked. "Sarajevo." No problem. We spoke a little about the past and the present. Then I asked about their plans. They told me, "We are waiting for the international community to build some factories." I said, "What did you do before the war?" "Agriculture." "Why don't you do it now?" "Oh no," they said. "The international community is guilty. They had the power to stop the war. They have to build." I asked them, "What about your education?" "It's too late for education. The international community is guilty, now they have to take care of us." They are un-educated, but all of them have worked in agriculture; this part of Bosnia is known for its fruits and vegetables. Now they're waiting for a factory that will never be built. They want to avoid the facts. One woman got a small grant and started to plant strawberries. But she is the exception.

Many people are afraid to talk about real problems, and the media in Bosnia won't talk about trauma or the women from Srebrenica trying to build houses for themselves. We aren't ready to speak about the past. We feel as if what's happened has happened, and that's that. People get angry at me when I talk about it. To me, if I bring it into the present I also bring it into the future. People don't want to do the work to move forward. They won't grieve because they can't tolerate the feelings it brings up. Revisiting trauma brings up humiliation and pain. People would rather stay blocked than speak about it and try to move through it. An organization of women from Srebrenica is trying to build houses in Sarajevo for themselves, and the media won't talk about it. Someone told these women the Dutch government would give them aid, but that didn't happen.

Facing genocide, the only choice is to try to survive. Keep going. Trust yourself. Know your own value system. Otherwise you're lost and can be manipulated. Americans don't realize it can happen to them. If it happened in Bosnia, Iraq, and Somalia, it can happen anywhere. It can enter your own country. If children aren't taught about peace, they will be faced with war.

*"What I know in my bones is that I forgot to
take time to remember what I know.
The world is holy. We are holy. All life is holy.
Daily prayers are delivered on the lips of breaking waves,
the whisperings of grasses, the shimmering of leaves."*
— Terry Tempest Williams

# Chapter 10
# Vjekoslav Saje
# Transcendence

*"Bosnia and its people are so beautiful."*

Vjekoslav Saje (Vee-yáyk-o-slav Sáh-hay) is an appealing, emotionally labile man. He was in his early forties at the time of our first interview. "Vjeko," as he is affectionately called, went from laughing to crying in one minute. He is a man of heart. Tears flow freely, then he'll break into laughter, remembering that the days of war are over, that everyone is safe, and they "made it through." Like many in Bosnia, Vjeko is multilingual and multicultural. He speaks fluent English. Born to a Roman Catholic family with a Croat mother and a Slovene father, he is married to Azra, a Bosniak, and they have one daughter, Irma, a successful fashion designer in Sarajevo. One of his great-grandmothers was a Hungarian Jew, and another was Austrian. His grandfather was Austrian. In alignment with his mixed heritage, Vjeko directs the Inter

Religious Dialogue in Sarajevo, an organization that Landrum Bolling,[67] someone I also knew well, helped him found.

A man of faith and courage, Vjeko appreciates the good and the humorous. Even during the darkest days, he found reasons to laugh. I would call his view of life *transcendent*, and even *self*-transcendent. Martin Seligman, the founding father of positive psychology, and his colleague, Christopher Peterson, describe transcendence as "reaching beyond the self … to embrace part or all of the larger universe. The prototype of this strength category is spirituality, variously defined but always referring to a belief in and commitment to the transcendent (nonmaterial) aspects of life—whether they be called universal, ideal, sacred, or divine."[68] Though all of the centerposts involve surpassing the self and its personal concerns, Vjeko's (like Sabiha's and Vahidin's) involved a deeply felt spiritual component. Vjeko never denied the horrors that surrounded him, but he also saw the beauty of Bosnia, listened to music, and snuggled in with his neighbors. He was able to keep the bigger picture in mind, even as he and his family focused on survival. Vjeko loves sensuous, lengthy, warm, song-filled Bosnian parties. "A good party is when you sit and eat a lot," he says, laughing infectiously. "They feed us nonstop, but we stay thin. Take *cevapćići* (a

---

[67] Landrum Bolling worked as a journalist in the early 1940s, when he spent time in the former Yugoslavia covering World War II and met Tito. He was later the president of Earlham College in Richmond, Indiana (the college I attended). After that, he became head of the Lilly Endowment Fund, then president and rector of the Tantur Ecumenical Institute in Jerusalem, and later an ambassador to Mercy Corps in Bosnia. Landrum Bolling was also one of my father's best friends. Vjeko's and my common Landrum connection was one example of the synchronicities that connected us. Landrum "saved my life" too, metaphorically, at a tough period during it. To me, this is an example of connections all around the world. Dr. Bolling died in January 2018 at the age of 104. He was described in a headline about his obituary as a "college president, peace activist, and presidential go-between." *Washington Post*, January 30, 2018.
[68] Peterson and Seligman, *Character Strengths*, 519.

lamb-and-beef combination prepared with delicate spices and eaten between slices of fresh, warm Bosnian bread or filo, or a fluffy flatbread called *lepina*. Cevapčiči is sold in small shops throughout Bosnia). I buy mine in in Baščaršija. There's this smell that probably goes back to instincts we had in the cave," and again he roars with laughter.

*Here is Vjekoslav Saje, in his own words:*
For 500 years, Sarajevans appreciated each other's cultures. Jews settled here after being expelled from Spain and Portugal, and they were welcomed by the Turkish administration. They never lived in ghettos here but were part of the city and community. They didn't have to change their names. People from Austria and the Czech Republic came here to mine and deal in commodities. Part of my family came during the Austrian fire. I was raised in this city, which for centuries was multicultural and multiethnic. In apartment buildings all around Sarajevo, everyone had mixed backgrounds. Some were pure Muslim, some were pure Croat, but we would still communicate and share Christmas and Ramadan. Before the war, I rarely noticed religion or nationality. Our focus was on human relations. We would boast that Bosnia was a small America. For intellectuals, the war was a total surprise.

The day before the war began, my daughter and I were skiing. On our way back to Sarajevo, we saw tanks on the road and then heard the news on TV that Sarajevo was being shelled. The UN came but didn't act. The Yugoslav army was well-equipped. Most of the officers were Serbs, and they silently and secretly took over all the armed forces. Through our taxes, we Bosnians had invested in the tanks and the snipers that attacked us! In just a few days, we were unable to leave Yugoslavia.[69]

---

[69] Vjekoslav still calls his home country "Yugoslavia."

The TV tower was among the first targets. They hit it with guided missiles. This was the beginning of the real siege; we were cut off from the world. TV workers put up small transmitters so we could get pictures again, but batteries were hard to find. Soon, even candles were hard to find. When we ran out of those, we made lamps with cotton and oil. People would read books by those lamps until they had to burn books for fuel.

Destroying bridges, burning books, these are the worst of times in human history. Try to imagine you live in Maryland and someone decides that all Presbyterians have to go to Virginia and Mennonites have to go to Delaware. If you're a Mennonite or a Presbyterian, you're forced to go. Serbs surreptitiously marked our houses with B's (for Bosniak) or H's (for Hvrastka, i.e. Croats). The Serb army came and took people out of their homes, according to the B's and H's. We were fighting for survival. The only safe place was in the trenches we dug, and we'd crawl from place to place. The city was defended by boys and girls fighting tanks. Many of them were killed.

My uncle stayed in Ilidža[70] to watch over his house. He was immediately taken to a camp. For two months, we fought to get him out. Some Serb friends helped us negotiate, and finally he was free, but he never recovered. They had tortured him; we saw the marks. They extinguished cigarettes on his hand. He was completely humiliated. They didn't harm him as much physically as psychologically. The effect was terrible. For six months, he lived with us while we looked for a place he could stay. It was hard because we lived in an attic and heard shells dropping all the time. So we moved him to the basement. Then our whole family lived in the basement.

---

[70] Ilidža is a town in central Bosnia-Herzegovina, famous for the natural beauty of its surroundings and historical tradition dating back to Neolithic times. Sarajevo International Airport is nearby, as is the famous Vrelo Bosne Spring.

Eventually, everyone in the building lived in the basement. It was fun in a way because when someone came back from the city, they would tell stories. It wasn't normal, but the communal sharing was precious.

*It was not Serbs and Muslims fighting, but good and evil fighting.*[71]

I don't want to put all Serbs in the same pot. During the war, our Serb neighbor helped my wife and me carry water. Another Serb woman helped the older people in our building, and she still lives there. Many of our country's actors are Serbs who stayed in the city and risked their lives along with ours. We were in hiding, but we attended the theater to see them, to continue enjoying life even in this confined space.

In the first years of the war, we were in the basement with our neighbors most of the time. I would always try to get my daughter down, and she would go back up. Kids are difficult to contain. That was the biggest stress. You have to take care of yourself, and you also have to think of everyone else: your kids, your wife, and your neighbors. There was heavy shelling. It was very close and always unexpected. The third year, one day we were about to leave our neighbors' house. There was a song on the radio, and I said to my wife, "Let's stay and listen." We did, and staying there saved our lives. There was a terrible shelling in front of the building. Our neighbor went out to buy cigarettes, and he was killed. We could have been with him. Another day while digging a trench, the guy beside me was killed, and I survived. Why was I chosen to survive? I thought about this a lot and almost blamed myself. In the fourth year, somehow we got used to the shelling. It was like rain. There was still fear, but it lessened. We prayed with our neighbors and sometimes we

---

[71] I put this phrase in italics because it demonstrates Vjekoslav's ability to focus on the bigger picture, right in the middle of the evil all around him. This is a transcendent quality.

even went to St. Anthony's Church. It was comforting to go to church, because at the beginning of the war, we wondered if there even was a God.

During one shelling, I was heading home, fighting block by block to get to my house, and I almost lost it. I thought, "Maybe we all deserve this somehow, perhaps we were unfaithful." That was a moment of weakness. I realized later that this kind of thinking could have been my demise. If I thought we deserved this evil for deserting God, I weakened my ability to fight against the evil. Before the war, we were a secular, socialist society. The communists made a big mistake in not allowing religion. Communist ideas are not all bad. They are basically the ideas of Jesus. But we lost certain values during the communist time. People did not appreciate religion. Some people were religious, but it was considered weird. If I went to church, I couldn't share it with my friends. During the war, my faith sustained me. One time at church, a woman was singing during the service. She sang so beautifully. She was singing a very high note—sustaining it beautifully—when a shell exploded very close by. She just continued singing.

During the war, we had a friend in Los Angeles who would have taken us in. Since my grandmother was a Jew, the Jewish community here could have put us on a flight, but when someone from the Jewish community called and asked us to confirm the flight, I couldn't do it. Bosnia and its people are so beautiful. This beauty is why I stayed. The juxtaposition of beauty with destruction can happen anywhere. No one is exempt. I'm glad we stayed, but I am not sure I would still be glad if someone from my family had been killed.

In 1994, my daughter, Irma, asked if she could go to Austria; we had family there. I was working with the UN and I could have gotten out easily, but I wasn't allowed to get my daughter out. So we planned her escape. She would crawl out through a tunnel underneath Sarajevo. Her mother was at the tunnel entry, and I was on the other side. A Serb guard accompanied her halfway through, and then she was on her own. It took all day, and I didn't know when or whether she would make it through. She had to walk about four miles through underground shelling. After she and I connected, we had to go over Mount Igman at night. It was extremely dangerous. Irma would look back over the mountain and say, "This is hell. I don't think I'll ever come back." She was right. It was hell—the shells and the sniping.

Crossing the mountains to Split, Croatia, was an incredible adventure. It took us three days to get there, normally a half-hour journey. We hitchhiked at night. There were checkpoints all along the way. Finally, a guy stopped and asked what we were doing out on the road at night. He invited us to stay at his house, as the shelling continued. Thank God we stayed in that village. We would have died if we'd been on the road. Finally, we got to Italy, but it was impossible to get a visa for Austria. We tried everywhere—Rome, Bologna. They said we had to get the visa in our home country, in Sarajevo. So we called my uncle, and he came by car and met us in Treblisi, on the border of Austria and Italy. We put Irma in the trunk, and he drove her to Austria. She finished high school there. That was 1995, when the war was basically over. Eventually she did come back.

It's difficult to realize that evil does exist and that there are people who want to harm you. I still sometimes find it hard to believe. I once read, "We laugh at Fascism, until it's too late." We were facing the forces of evil, supported by the enormous power of the Yugoslav army. Unfortunately, during the war, the conflict was not interpreted as good fighting evil; it was seen as fighting among three tribes. Though it's hard, I believe in the power of good to overcome evil.

For a while we were totally cut off from the world, but then an Italian organization helped bring letters in and we started to feel better. We were connected to the outside world again. Then the banks began to reopen and somehow money was brought in from the outside. Though food prices were still through the roof—sugar was $50 a kilo—we could always forage for nettles. It became our favorite food.[72] I made nettle tea, nettle stew, and nettle pie. Because of this grace, I was able to keep my faith and believe that good does prevail over evil.

It also helped to be in touch with others who were struggling. We never lost hope. Thousands of outsiders of good will came to Bosnia during the war. Vanessa Redgrave came through the tunnel three times during the siege and experienced with us what we were suffering. I took it as a sign that there is good in the world—people who cared—and it helped us not sink in despair in those times of incredible turmoil. People coming from the outside helped us feel connected, especially in our darkest moments.

Healing is a lengthy and ongoing process. It doesn't always have to wait until after the war. People can heal even during the most awful moments. It isn't guaranteed, but people can heal from the most horrible events. Healing meant going to the theater. That was a courageous act. You could be killed on the way. Landrum Bolling, the director-at-large of Mercy Corps in Washington, DC, came in 1995 and stayed for two years. He saved my life. I met Landrum at St. Andrew's Church with David Steele, and he suggested we do interreligious work together. So, I left the UN and began working with him. That's how my project, Interreligious Dialogues, got started.

A courageous journalist was the first to discover the detention camps, a breakthrough that was the beginning of the end. This is a lesson to the world—we need to inform each other what is really happening. Real information can prevent the worst. We need courageous journalists, people to spread

---

[72] It turns out that nettles are known as Nature's Milk. They are the most complete herb there is. In folklore, they are thought to be the breast milk of Mother Nature. Thanks to herbalist Kimberly McKnight for this information and to Jungian analyst Muriel McMahon for sharing it with me.

the word. Actors and celebrities can also do a lot. After this journalist's report, Clinton acted. Then Tudjman, as the president of Croatia, took over, and eventually the reasonable Croats had no choice but to take a portion of Bosnia and annex it to Croatia. Milošević finally made a deal with Tudjman and took at least half of Bosnia from him. For 500 years, before there were nation-states, people lived in the big kingdom of Bosnia. It was a huge surprise to the people of Bosnia to have something like this repeated at the end of the twentieth century.

The American response was a little late. We were disappointed in the UN, too. Kofi Annan allowed horrible things to happen here and in Iraq and Rwanda. He was too focused on his own career. Many people in the UN are more concerned with their own interests than others' needs. The UN should be transformed into an organization that prevents war and violent conflicts and is more connected with local organizations. I wouldn't say the UN did nothing, but so much more could have been done.

Most Bosnians appreciate what the Clinton administration did for us, but after a crisis subsides, outsiders forget. Our economic situation is not developing as it could. I expected more investment here from other countries. Instead, we have Jerry Springer on our TVs. While I know he is not typical of the US, others do not. Bosnians' view of Americans now is mixed, given their exporting of TV programs like Jerry Springer's.[73]

My view of human nature has changed. I am disappointed in the materialistic attitudes of people, not just in America but everywhere. Now we have malls in Sarajevo, which are destroying the small shops, our way of life and the soul of the city. This is true in Italy and Spain, too. For many people, going to the mall is like going to a shrine. It's both

---

[73] Jerry Springer, a former US politician, was a tabloid TV talk show host.

worship and entertainment, something you have to do on the weekends. How can a person resist? In a capitalistic economy, you fight to get more. I notice many of my American friends don't have time to *live*. They struggle to get a mansion and then have no time to enjoy it. They're exhausted. The US is just rich communism; things are under the control of certain forces. US citizens are more limited than they realize. They think they are free, but they aren't.

The war happened because some people didn't want to accept other cultures. To feel safe, they wanted to dominate; they didn't want to share. They wanted to insulate and isolate. I facilitated a teleseminar from Sarajevo about the Muslim viewpoint. We called one mufti and imams from all over Bosnia. The mufti said, "At this point, the question for Muslims is how to deal with all these problems the world is facing, not only in Bosnia. One solution is isolation. Another is assimilation, which is frightening, not only for Muslims." He suggested integration, stressing this to his imams, and most of them accepted his message.

This is important because we have problems with people introducing a new kind of Islam here in Bosnia. They are called Mahabis (Wahhabis). Some of them are extreme and connected with terrorists. You see women wearing veils, not just here, but everywhere. The problems are not as big here as in Germany. People say Bosnia is a place where terrorism might occur, but it's unlikely, because the core of Muslim hierarchy in Bosnia is strongly against it. The extremists are limited in their actions. We have freedom of speech. You can't just kill people or put them in prison here. You have to live with them and not let them dominate.

Evil is a constant possibility. We need to create a structure where evil will not prevail. We need to make rules and regulations not to enable it. The desire to dominate and the desire to take from others are evil. I'm not only talking about Bosnia. When I saw the towers collapsing in New York, I went out of my mind. I was in New York just two months earlier; I knew there were people in those buildings. Before the war, I lived and worked with a Bosnian company in Baghdad for five years. I know people in Baghdad. My best friend at the time was a Palestinian. I was also in Israel, and I know that Israelis and Palestinians are both suffering. There are so many issues.

People who are not successful in peacetime become extremely successful during war. War made Hitler, Milošević, and Karadzić. There was a time in our history when people were in positions of power because of nepotism and other sorts of corruption. Karadzić lived in Sarajevo, but he hated it. He never became a real Sarajevan. He probably couldn't deal with those who wanted coexistence. He was thinking only of his own tribe.

The other day I was watching a young Serb pop singer on TV, and he said, "We're going to Istanbul. We were conquered by the Turks 500 years ago, and this time we will win." The desire for revenge is the basis of conflict. This guy is still thinking about his ancestors suffering, and he wants to take revenge. There's a lot of work to do. Karadzić is still a hero for many Serbs. A universal standard of behavior is needed, with effective, structured, and strong principles. The Serbian pop star is still obsessing about revenge after 500 years, about how Muslims conquered his country. The seed of yet another conflict is that he doesn't forgive.

To quote Landrum, "Forgiveness means giving up all hope for a better past." You can forgive if you give up all hope of changing the past. Even God cannot change the past. We can try to make a better present and future with our friends and family by disseminating this idea. We can take small steps for a better future, a better world. Everything counts.

Appreciative Inquiry is a good thing. Cynthia Samson and her colleagues introduced it in Bosnia. It's a method of conflict prevention. Cynthia was my teacher at Eastern Mennonite University, a Christian school in Virginia. EMU focuses on peace, service, sustainability, community, and cross-cultural studies. She was a member of the team that launched Appreciative Inquiry. You focus on positive aspects of a subject. It can be applied to a business, a school, or a city. It was used in the schools in Chicago in a project called "Chicago Hope," or "Imagine Chicago." They taught Appreciative Inquiry to young people and had them dream about a better city. Chicago was in bad shape, and the young people came up with ideas and processed them, and now they are actually making a better Chicago. We also used Appreciative Inquiry in our seminar in the Muslim community.[74]

We are developing a network of peacemakers. I wrote a chapter in the book *Religion and Reconciliation in Bosnia*, by Paul Mojzes.[75] Recently, I facilitated seminars with David Steele[76] in Macedonia. We organized summer camps for kids and founded a school in Kozarać.[77] The experience and knowledge of a region should not be lost. I can share some of what I know so that people don't repeat the same steps that led us to war. I'm discussing this with Landrum since he's very connected in the Middle East. He says that peacemakers must be financed to fight evil. War is financed in huge amounts, so why not give the same amount of funding to peacemakers?

My daughter is graduating from the Academy of Fine Arts in Sarajevo. She won first prize in France for fashion

---

[74] See "What is Appreciative Inquiry?" in David L. Cooperrider and Diana Whitney, *Appreciative Inquiry: A Positive Revolution in Change* (San Francisco: Berrett-Koehler, 2005).

[75] Paul Mojzes, *Religion and the War in Bosnia* (New York: Oxford University Press, 1998).

[76] David Steele earned a PhD in Christian ethics and practical theology from the University of Edinburgh, where he wrote a dissertation on a theological assessment of conflict resolution theory and practice. He is the author of numerous publications on faith-based peacebuilding, and he facilitates conflict transformation programs in violence-prone areas of interethnic and sectarian conflict.

[77] Kozarać is a town in northwestern Bosnia-Herzegovina, six miles east of Prijedor and twenty-seven miles west of Banja Luka.

design, and she is hopeful about our city and country. Two years ago, the Bosnian Pontanima Interfaith Choir sang with the orchestra from Banja Luka, the largest city of the Serb-majority Republika Srpska. *Pontanima* means "bridge of souls." It's Latin. They sang traditional songs of all faiths. It was beautiful to hear Muslim and Serb songs being sung in a Catholic church. No one was thinking, "Where are these singers from, Republika Srpska or Bosnia-Herzegovina?"[78]

Of course, we still face evil. We will always have to deal with that, but distinctions are breaking down. Things are changing. U-2 was here after the war and people from Banja Luca came by the busload. We had great feasts together. Now we have freedom of speech again, and young people are working together to create cultural events.

A young guy on TV last night was talking about our special way of life in Sarajevo. It's unique in the world, he said. The food is wonderful, the people are friendly, we accept each other. It's a vibrant, real city, and it's wonderful to live here. We have such a beautiful country. We need to work harder to ensure peace.

---

[78] The Ponanima Interfaith Choir won the Pax Christi International Peace Award in 2011. https://disciples.org/overseas-ministries/bosnian-choir-receives-international-peace-award/

# Part III
# Conclusion

*"Love and kindness are the antithesis of evil."*
— C.G. Jung

# Chapter 11
# Making It Home

Chapter One, "The Centerpost," began with the image of Odysseus lashed to the mast of his ship to resist the dangerous and compelling lure of the Sirens. This image came to me as I was reflecting on these interviews a few years after they had taken place.

How had each of these wonderful people made it through? This profound image was guiding *me*—not just Odysseus and the survivors of the war in Bosnia-Herzegovina—in the quest to make it through and ultimately, to make it home. The word itself—*centerpost*—was etched on the image. At the time, I did not think about Odysseus' journey, or its archetypal implications. Odysseus's journey is ultimately a voyage home to his sweetheart, his beloved, his wife from whom he'd been away for twenty years, his place in society, and his son who had grown up during his absence.[79] These Bosnian survivors' stories represent just such a grand, noble, arduous, soul-searing and ultimately archetypal journey home.

Home itself is also an archetype. The heartfelt feeling of "home" is found everywhere, in all human societies. Home is where we belong. In the best of circumstances, home is where we are safe, accepted, loved, and surrounded by familiar objects and people. Ideally, when we walk in the door of our home, someone greets us, is glad to see us. It may also have to do with the land, what it smells like, looks like, the comfort of its contours, all of which we may have taken for granted

---

[79] Many thanks to Dr. Bonnie Damron, who helped me understand this.

before losing it. Without it and the belonging our home, families and neighbors confer on us, we feel rootless, lost, and ungrounded. Many are in that condition today.

In his book *To Bless the Space Between Us: A Book of Blessings,* the beloved late Irish poet and teacher John O'Donohue writes about home this way:

"Home is where the heart is. It stands for the sure center where individual life is shaped and from where it journeys forth. What it ultimately intends is that each of its individuals would develop the capacity to be at home in themselves. This is something that is usually overlooked, but it is a vital requirement in the creativity and integrity of individual personality. It has to do with the essence of a person, their sense of their own inner ground."[80]

When we are pulled away from our home, we lose something essential to our sense of self, our identity, who we actually *are*. We may not have been aware of it before, but when our home is blown to smithereens or we are forced to leave it, the cost is great. With the coerced loss of home, many people's sense of identity is dashed to pieces, and fragments of a former self are left to focus on survival. How can we make it home to ourselves, our souls, our families, our purpose, and our passion in a world full of chaos and confusion?

In his book on blessings, O'Donohue addresses the question this way: "When a person is at home in his life, he always has a clear instinct about the shape of outer situations; even in the midst of confusion, he can discern the traces of a path forward."[81]

O'Donohue is pointing to something deeper than a physical home. He is describing the essence of what grounded our narrators and can ground us in the midst of turmoil. By clinging to this "clear instinct," this centerpost as best we can,

---

[80] O'Donohue, *To Bless the Space*, 82.
[81] O'Donohue, *To Bless the Space*, 82.

some of what has been lost can be restored. But only an *inner home* can stabilize us when nothing else is stable, when the earth herself might open up and swallow us, or when our neighbors turn into savages, as happened in Bosnia in the early 1990s. As I asked each interviewee, "How did you make it through *that?*" the underlying question, not yet known to me, was how did you make it home, how did you make it all the way through? This is a book about Bosnia. And it is also about everyone. A woman who attended a talk I gave about this book said, with tears running down her face, "Oh my God, these people are just like us."

This book is about survivors of genocide and of ethnic cleansing. And yet, it is also about us. The insights and qualities manifested by these eight inspiring women and men also apply to each of us in our daily lives, and not just in extreme moments. And now, as our world faces destruction from many sources, including human ignorance and tyrannical governments, how can we make it all the way through to goodness, hope, purpose, making a difference, and yes, happiness?

Three thresholds come to mind that were prominent in the interviews: "thresholds," because they seem to be portals to the soul. The first and perhaps the most important was the centerpost they each held onto during the war. The second is connection to others, often hard to find in a lonely society. And the third is forgiveness. "Forgiveness" and "connection" are profoundly linked. Through forgiveness ("unburdening ourselves") receiving or giving kindness, we rejoin the human race and reconnect with others, and it's through our sense of connectedness that we are given the grace to forgive.

*Connection*

Before the war, Bosnia was a family-oriented society. Our interviewees and most Bosnian inhabitants experienced strong family ties and community with others. Prewar, their country's motto was "Brotherhood and Unity," which their government fostered. Each interviewee actually experienced this. The Bosnians interviewed for this book valued and maintained connections with others throughout the war and with their own centerposts. For these particular survivors, even war and genocide did not bring about complete disconnection from their families, friends, and some neighbors, nor did it sever them from their souls, values, or integrity.

Salih rescued person after person wounded on Sniper Alley, risking his life while racing to their side, doing CPR, calling ambulances, and accompanying them to the hospital. His actions represented connection after connection with others.

Marijana and Sabiha created an inspired ritual reframing the lives of babies born of rape. These babies, Sabiha declared, were "a gift from God." In this ritual, Marijana and Sabiha sacralized children and their mothers who might have been cut off from their families and banned from society.

Jakob embraced his whole Sarajevo community, Jewish and non-Jewish, as he led them in celebrating La Benevolencia, establishing three pharmacies, and offering opportunities for elders to leave Sarajevo while there was still time.

Senka remained bonded to her husband and children even when she did not know where her husband was or even whether he was alive. She never gave up. Later, she found his bones and gave him a proper burial, establishing yet another ongoing relationship.

Milka suffered over being a member of the perpetrator group, but she stayed in touch with her students, her own children, and her mother, and later made reparations with Vahidin and other Bosniak friends. During and after the Karuna Center trainings, she reunited with her deep self through tears of remorse.

Vjekoslav stayed connected to his family, friends, and neighbors living together in their apartment building basement, hunting for nettles, making nettle tea, soup, and stew for everyone, and attending the theater and underground concerts. Though his centerpost is transcendence, one of the qualities that surfaced often in him was joy. Joy is an emotion of deep connection to others, even if the others are not physically present. Joy is the opposite of gloom and helps to dispel it.

Vahidin's story of finally coming to forgiveness after years of rage and thoughts of vengeance is one of profound connection and disconnection at the same time, ending up with links to the whole world.

The hardest form of openness is with those who have inflicted harm on you, the perpetrators. It's difficult to get beyond our revulsion toward them and consider them part of the human family. When Vahidin admitted he'd rather be a victim than a victimizer, he was recognizing something that is often hidden; that the suffering of a perpetrator can be deeper than that of a victim. This realization was the beginning of Vahidin's journey back to wholeness, as he regained the ability to connect with some Serbs.

When a *perpetrator* is able to *feel* what he or she has done to others, it reconnects them to other people, and especially to their victims.

## Forgiveness

Lynne McTaggart writes about this eloquently, telling the story of German theologian Geiko Müller-Fahrenholz and his book *The Art of Forgiveness*.[82] Like many Germans too young to have experienced World War II directly, Müller-Fahrenholz carried a deep sense of guilt and regret for his country's terrible legacy. He began considering forgiveness from both the perpetrators' and the victims' points of view. He considered wrongdoing a mutual bondage between perpetrator and victim, including even the most minor transgressions, which, he believes, establish a distorted relationship between

---

[82] Geiko Müller–Fahrenholz, *The Art of Forgiveness: Theological Reflections on Healing and Reconciliation* (New York: World Council of Churches, 1997).

two people.[83] His book includes remarkable examples of the profound bonding that can result from true forgiveness, which necessarily includes a perpetrator's deeply felt experience of the harm that he has caused.

McTaggert writes:
Müller-Fahrenholz tells the story of a group of old Germans who had fought in Belarussia as part of Hitler's army during World War II. They decided to return to the country in 1994, fifty years later, in an attempt to make amends for what they'd done as young men. Their visit occurred after the Chernobyl nuclear accident, so they offered to build a home for children affected by the disaster. Toward the end of their stay they visited a war memorial at Chatyn. That evening, full of the memories brought up by the visit, the Germans wanted to share the experience with their Belarusian hosts.

"After a round of very personal toasts, one of the Germans, still clearly overcome by his visit to Chatyn, stood up to talk about his own history as a young soldier. He began describing his own suffering in a Russian prison-of-war camp, but abruptly stopped. He excused himself for a moment and then suddenly broke down. He said how deeply sorry he was for what he personally had done to the Russians and also apologized on behalf of his country.

"He tried to say that it must never happen again, but his voice again broke, and he had to sit down because he was sobbing so hard. Everyone in the room, even the young people who had no experience of war, was weeping.

---

[83] Quoted in Lynn McTaggert, *The Bond: Connecting Through the Space Between Us.* (New York: Free Press, 2011), 174-175.

174

"After a few minutes a Belarusian woman of similar age stood up, crossed the room, and kissed him.

"At the moment of the German's genuine act of confession, the full hurt was acknowledged and the dignity of everyone in the room was restored. For the old woman, forgiveness was sparked by the sudden realization that the pain of others—even the pain of the perpetrator—was also her pain and that of every one of the victims."

"This moment of connecting to the other's pain is the transcendent aspect of any relationship," writes Müller-Fahrenholz, "offering 'a spark of courage to open up, that moment of daring and trusting which causes the heart to jump over the fence.'[84] Ultimately it is this sudden merging that tears down 'the dividing walls' between us."[85]

A global example of healing through a deep listening process, not unlike the one in the example above, is the Truth and Reconciliation process in South Africa, which brought perpetrators to justice and had them *listen* to the people they hurt. Some of the perpetrators had a conversion of the heart, even some of the most hardened ones, as they were forced to hear and face what they had done. If perpetrators witness the suffering they caused, sometimes they *feel* what they did, which can begin the process of restoring them to themselves and to the human community. If that happens, this can help their victims connect with them, although this is not necessary for victims to unburden themselves.

---

[84] Geiko Müller–Fahrenholz, "On Shame and Hurt in the Life of Nations: A German Perspective," *Irish Quarterly Review* 78 (1989), 127-35. Quoted in McTaggert, 176.
[85] McTaggert, *Bond*, 176.

Hurting, maiming, and killing others hurts *us*, ourselves, as we saw with Müller-Fahrenholz's story of the German man who had been a young soldier during World War II. Staying in touch with our own souls is difficult in a world already filled with suffering and pain, but it is necessary to stay connected to our pain and that of others, to hope, and to each other, because connection to each other is a prerequisite to making it through.[86] This does not mean befriending our betrayers or our abusers. It is deeper than that. The word "connection" relates to these Bosnians' actions during the war, representing a commitment to caring for their families, friends, neighbors, and ultimately their society.

Although we did not use the word "forgiveness" in the Karuna Center trainings, nor did we introduce the concept, four of the eight interviewees mentioned the word themselves during their interviews. These are four survivors of *genocide* who brought up the idea of forgiveness, so we know in no uncertain terms how important it must be. We also know that it's easier to forgive if the perpetrator has some recognition of what he or she has done. Although this isn't necessary for us to "unburden ourselves" (Vahidin's definition of forgiveness), it helps.

This is congruent with what Vahidin told me in our interview. He said he was glad that the Serb who came to him and told him he couldn't sleep, actually couldn't sleep. Vahidin believed this Serb man needed to suffer over what he had done and he, Vahidin, was glad the man was having nightmares. Eventually, Vahidin could embrace this man fully, but not until the man suffered. This might sound like Vahidin still wanted revenge, but that isn't what he meant. Vahidin was hoping for

---

[86] See The Shift Network (https://theshiftnetwork.com) for a remarkable online community composed of world-renowned thought leaders pointing the way to a better world. See, also, https://www.soundstrue.com for thought leaders leading us out of the doldrums of darkened, hate-filled and hopeless patterns of thought and emotion.

a full healing for the man, and he knew that only by feeling and suffering over what he had done, could he heal.

Marijana Senjak witnessed moments of forgiveness throughout the war but said that forgiving the perpetrator is not crucial to a person's recovery.[87] "The crucial thing," she said, "is to forgive yourself and to find some spiritual meaning in your life."

When Vjekoslav described the young Serb musician pop singer saying his jazz group was going to Istanbul and they would finally win and conquer, Vjeko added: "This Serbian pop singer is still thinking of revenge. After 500 years, he is still thinking of how Muslims conquered his country. The base, the seed for conflict, is that he didn't forgive." The main point here is Vjeko's comment, *"The base, the seed for conflict, is that he didn't forgive."*

Sabiha stressed throughout her interview that although for her, forgiveness is very important, she would never urge it on anyone else. Yet, at the end of her interview, she said, "Forgiveness opens the door for our soul." I understand her to mean that *our* hard-heartedness is released by the act of forgiving; *our* hard-heartedness, the ones who were wounded and are justified in resenting.

Forgiveness is a long process, as Desmond and Mpho Tutu point out in their book *The Art of Forgiveness*, but in the end, it is we, the forgivers, who benefit. Then, so does the world, since every act and thought of each of us influences the whole. Archbishop Tutu's famous remark, "Without forgiveness, there is no future," brings up the question again: What *is* forgiveness? Is it even possible in the face of horrific violence and abuse?

"Unburdening oneself" means freedom to be oneself and live one's life, not shackled by chronic hatred and resentment.

---

[87] Marijana cited Ellen Bass' and Laura Davis' seminal book on healing from abuse *The Courage to Heal*, when she said that.

177

If we forgive in the way these thinkers suggest, we can wrestle free from resentment, bitterness, chronic anger or hurt. We can come to realize we are responsible for what we do, but not for what is done to us, and we can release the latter. Forgiveness is a long spiritual process, but it is ultimately worth it. It grants a more hopeful view of humanity than ongoing resentments does. But is it realistic?

Let's remember Vahidin's working definition of forgiveness here: "unburdening ourselves." It is not about being gullible, condoning terrible wrongs, or setting oneself up for further abuse and conquest. It is about becoming free ourselves so we can lead others to this place of inner freedom and together make a better world. If we don't find a way to release ourselves from resentment, we end up contributing to the massive problems from which our world is suffering.

*The Intergenerational Transmission of Suffering, Revisited*

When we understand that the suffering of survivors can even be transmitted culturally and neurologically to their children and grandchildren down through the generations,[88] we see how difficult true forgiveness is.

New research suggests that experiencing intense psychological trauma may have a genetic impact on a person's

---

[88] The *intergenerational transmission of trauma* is the term used to describe a collective sense of injustice and woundedness, based on what happened to our forebears, sometimes centuries earlier. This term explains how trauma is transmitted even in the DNA of the children of survivors of the Holocaust. These children didn't go through the Holocaust themselves, but they suffer from it more deeply than they would by merely absorbing their parents' unhealed wounds. This understanding of the intergenerational transmission of trauma gives us even more impetus for forgiveness, seen as healing from a sense of injustice that inevitably results in a feeling of justification in punishing the aggressor for what their forebears did. Not forgiving obviously sets the stage for ongoing and unresolved conflict worldwide.

future children. A study examining the DNA of Holocaust survivors and their children found similar variations from the norm in both generations for genes associated with depression and anxiety disorders. The findings imply that children of individuals who experience profound stress in life may be more likely to develop stress or anxiety disorders themselves. "'The pattern—known as an epigenetic change because it affects the *expression* of the gene rather than the gene itself— suggests that profound stress in the older generation translated into an adaptation that passed on to the next,' said Dr. Rachel Yehuda, director of Mount Sinai's Traumatic Stress Studies Division and leader of the study. Scientists have long-known that parents pass genetic traits down to their children, but Yehuda's research suggests that life experiences can also produce chemical effects in DNA."[89]

To get beyond this, we must "do our work" on ourselves and be willing to change. If we do not "do our work," meaning suffer consciously the pain of our trauma and transform it, we will unconsciously and even biologically transmit it to others. Claude Anshin Thomas, the Vietnam War veteran who became a Buddhist monk writes, "It is ... our unhealed, unaddressed suffering that propels us to industrialized killing."[90]

---

[89] Similar research has been done into the effects of famine on later generations, as well as stress levels in the children of women who survived the September 11 attacks. Although the study involved just 32 Holocaust survivors and their offspring, Yehuda said the findings provide proof of the concept that could lead to more research into exactly how the changes occur. The findings may provide an explanation for why people like Karen Sonneberg struggle with anxiety and stress disorders despite having never experienced trauma themselves. Sonneberg's Jewish parents both suffered under Nazi oppression in Germany at a young age. She said many of her friends with similar backgrounds experienced similar struggles with anxiety. There were definitely challenges that quote unquote 'American' kids didn't seem to have experienced," Sonneberg said. From *PBS News Hour*, August 31, 2015.

[90] Thomas, *Hell's Gate*, 43.

Psychological "numbing" is Robert Jay Lifton's term for "unhealed, unaddressed suffering that propels us to industrialized killing." Being dangerously numb is how perpetrators perpetrate, and in the case of the Bosnian and other wars, the soldiers were often literally numb on alcohol or drugs. By "numbness," Lifton means not suffering our emotional wounds and scars *consciously*; not feeling them, avoiding the pain, denying it and acting it out on others instead. This unfelt suffering, Lifton's "numbness," can lead to an ability to stuff your neighbor into a gas oven and go home and have dinner. Awake, feeling people cannot do this. A bigger, more aware part of ourselves than the wounded one is the part that can forgive, and that is the one that will heal the world.

## Making It Home

Vahidin's interview contains nine statements about home. The most poignant shows him rejoicing to be home again after four years away as a refugee. "I wanted to scream, "I'm not a refugee anymore! It was like taking off a heavy coat, taking off a burden. I had my rights back!" For Vahidin, home represented the qualities named at the start of this chapter: belonging, acceptance, familiarity, and a deep sense of rootedness. Without it and living in a refugee camp, he lost all his rights, his hope, his connection with God, his purpose for living, and his sense of identity. By "home," he evokes his physical home and the end of his journey, like Odysseus, who likewise made it home in both senses of the word.

Odysseus's journey is really a love story. So, in the end, is our journey "home." The image of the mast that flashed into my mind that warm, fall afternoon a decade ago when I was contemplating the Bosnians' stories, was pregnant with symbolic meanings long buried in my own mind. These survivors clung to an internal rudder guiding them through horrific conditions, propelled by love, like Odysseus, allowing them to make it all the way through. This explains to me why the stories like those of these eight wonderful Bosnians are so gripping and have universal appeal. Wherever I present their stories, some people are in tears, able to identify with the soul-searing journey, even though most, of course, have not gone through genocide or war.

In St. Petersburg, Russia, after hearing my presentation, a psychotherapist commented that she had never believed she could be healed of her own trauma until she heard these stories. Another Russian participant, a psychoanalyst, also in tears, commented that these stories made him feel compassion for himself as he realized the vicarious trauma he had suffered working with trauma survivors in Chechnya. As trauma increases in our world—on many fronts and for many reasons, destructive and inhumane out-of-control authoritarian governments being one of them—stories like these can inspire us to stay close to ourselves, our centerposts, and to do what we can to weather the storm.

Ultimately, whatever we have been through, no matter how horrendous or even seemingly insignificant, we are all in this together.

Tommy Sands quotes Pete Seeger in his *Music of Healing:* "Even when we're torn asunder, Love will come again."[91]

And as Viktor Frankl wrote in *Man's Search for Meaning,* "I saw the truth as it is set into song by so many poets, proclaimed as the final wisdom by so many thinkers. The truth—that love is the ultimate and the highest goal to which man can aspire. Then I grasped the meaning of the greatest secret that human poetry and human thought and

---

[91] In Tommy Sands's *The Music of Healing.* Sands said he borrowed those words from Pete Seeger.

belief have to impart: *The salvation of man is through love and in love.* "[92]

These stories are offered to encourage forgiveness, connection, and ultimately *Making It Home* to love for all of us.

---

[92] Viktor Frankl, *Man's Search for Meaning* (Boston: Beacon Press, 2006), 37-38.

# Further Reading

## Spiritual and Psychological Resources

Frankl, Viktor. *Man's Search for Meaning*. (Boston: Beacon) 1959, 1962, 1984, 1992, 2006.

Hart, David L. *The Water of Life: Spiritual Renewal in the Fairy Tale*. (Canada, UK and USA: Fisher King Press) 2013.

Hunt, Swanee. *This Was Not Our War: Bosnian Women Reclaiming the Peace*. (Durham and London: Duke University Press) 2004.

Jung, C.G. *Memories, Dreams, Reflections*. (New York: Vintage Books, a Division of Random House) 1961, 1962, 1963.

Jung, C.G. *The Archetypes and the Collective Unconscious. Volume 9,1, of the Collected Works of C.G. Jung*. (New York: Bollingen Foundation, 1959; Princeton University Press) 1969.

Lear, Jonathan. *Radical Hope: Ethics in the Face of Cultural Devastation*. (Cambridge and London: Harvard University Press) 2006.

Mantz, Joshua. *The Beauty of a Darker Soul: Overcoming Trauma Through the Power of Human Connection*. (Austin, TX. Lioncrest) 2018.

Peterson, Christopher and Seligman, Martin. *Character Strengths and Virtues: A Handbook and Classification*. (New York: Oxford University Press) 2004. Copyright 2004 by

Values in Action Institute. Published by the American Psychological Association, Washington, DC. 2004.

Rogers, Annie. *A Shining Affliction: A Story of Harm and Healing in Psychotherapy.* (New York: Penguin Books) 1995.

## The Balkans

Cohen, Roger. *Hearts Grown Brutal: Sagas of Sarajevo.* (New York: Random House) 1998.

Glenny, Misha. *The Fall of Yugoslavia.* (London: Penguin Books) 1992, 1993, 1996.

Maas, Peter. *Love Thy Neighbor.* (New York: Knopf) 1996.

Neuffer, Elizabeth. *The Key to My Neighbor's House: Seeking Justice in Bosnia and Rwanda.* (New York: Picador Press) 2001.

Pond, Elizabeth. *Endgame in the Balkans: Regime Change, European Style.* (Washington, DC, The Brookings Institution) 2006.

## Evil

Buber, Martin. *Good and Evil.* (New York: Charles Scribner's Sons) 1952, 1953.

Deikman, Arthur. *The Wrong Way Home: Uncovering the Patterns of Cult Behavior in American Society.* (Boston: Beacon) 1990.

Kelman, Herbert C. and Hamilton, V. Lee. *Crimes of Obedience.* (New Haven: Yale University Press) 1989.

Lifton, Robert Jay. *Thought Reform and the Psychology of Totalism: A Study of "Brainwashing" in China.* (Chapel Hill, NC: University of North Carolina Press) 1989.

Peck, Scott. *People of the Lie: The Hope for Healing Human Evil.* (New York: Simon & Schuster) 1983.

Sanford, John A. *Evil: The Shadow Side of Reality.* (New York: Crossroad) 1988.

Staub, Ervin. *The Psychology of Good and Evil: Why Children, Adults, and Groups Help and Harm Others.* (Cambridge: Cambridge University Press) 2003.

Staub, Ervin. *The Roots of Evil: The Origins of Genocide and Other Group Violence* (New York: Cambridge University Press) 1989.

Stein, Murray. *Jung on Evil.* (Princeton: Princeton University Press) 1995.

Woodruff, Paul and Wilmer, Harry A. *Facing Evil: Light at the Core of Darkness.* (La Salle, IL: Open Court) 1988.

Zimbardo, Philip. *The Lucifer Effect: Understanding How Good People Turn Evil.* (New York: Random House) 2007.

# Genocide

Coloroso, Barbara. *Extraordinary Evil: A Short Walk to Genocide.* (New York: Nation Books) 2007.

Lifton, Robert Jay. *The Nazi Doctors: Medical Killing and the Psychology of Genocide.* (New York: Basic Books) 1986.

Post, Jerrold M. *Leaders and Their Followers in a Dangerous World: The Psychology of Political Behavior.* (Ithaca and London: Cornell University Press) 2004.

Power, Samantha. *A Problem from Hell: America and the Age of Genocide.* (New York: Basic Books) 2002.

Weine, Stevan M. *When History is a Nightmare: Lives and Memories of Ethnic Cleansing in Bosnia-Herzegovina.* (New Brunswick, NJ and London) 1999.

# Trauma

Bernstein, Jerome S. *Living in the Borderland: The Evolution of Consciousness and the Challenge of Healing Trauma.* (London: Routledge) 2005.

Cruz, Leonard and Buser, Steven. *A Clear and Present Danger: Narcissism in the Era of Donald Trump.* (Asheville, NC: Chiron Press) 2016.

Kalsched, Donald. *The Inner World of Trauma: Archetypal Defenses of the Personal Spirit.* (London and New York: Routledge) 1996.

Kalsched, Donald. *Trauma and the Soul: A Psycho-spiritual Approach to Human Development and its Interruption* (London: Routledge) 2013.

Herman, Judith Lewis. *Trauma and Recovery: The Aftermath of Violence—From Domestic Abuse to Political Terror.* (New York: Basic Books) 1992.

Levine, Peter A., PhD. *In an Unspoken Voice: How the Body Releases Trauma and Restores Goodness.* (Berkeley, CA., North Atlantic Books) 2010.

Levine, Peter A., PhD. *Trauma and Memory: Brain and Body in a Search for the Living Past.* (Berkeley, CA., North Atlantic Books) 2015.

Ogden, Pat, Minton, Kekuni, and Pain, Clare. *Trauma and the Body. A Sensorimotor Approach to Psychotherapy.* (New York: W.W. Norton & Co.) 2006.

Rogers, Annie G., PhD. *The Unsayable: The Hidden Language of Trauma.* (New York: Randon House) 2006. (New York and London: Ballantine Books, an imprint of Random House) 2007.

## War

Brock, Rita Nakashima and Lettini, Gabriella. *Soul Repair: Recovering from Moral Injury after War* (Boston: Beacon) 2012.

Grossman, Lt. Col. Dave. *On Killing: The Psychological Cost of Learning to Kill in War and Society.* (New York, Boston, London: Back Bay Books, Little Brown & Co.) 1995, 1996, 2009.

Swanson, David. *War is a Lie.* (Charlottesville, VA: Just World Books) 2016.

Tick, Edward, PhD. *War and the Soul: Healing Our Nation's Veterans from Post-traumatic Stress Disorder.* (Wheaton, IL: Quest Books) 2005.

# Violence

Bailie, Gil. *Violence Unveiled: Humanity at the Crossroads.* (New York: Crossroad) 1997.

Gilligan, James, M.D. *Violence: Reflections on a National Epidemic.* (New York: Random House) 1996.

Keen, Sam. *Faces of the Enemy: Reflections of the Hostile Imagination.* (San Francisco: Harper & Row) 1986.

Schmookler, Andrew Bard. *Out of Weakness: Healing the Wounds That Drive Us to War.* (New York: Bantam Books) 1998.

# Acknowledgments

It takes a community to write a book. I have had helpers in so many different forms. First and foremost, I thank the eight interviewees who generously shared their stories so we can all learn from their heartrending experiences. Vjekoslav Saje, in addition to sharing his story, patiently read and corrected the history chapter and helped me understand crucial terms like *ethnic cleansing*.

Paula Green, the founder and director emerita of the Karuna Center for Peacebuilding (KCP), is a brilliant peace-builder and winner of the Dalai Lama's award for unsung heroes of compassion. It was Paula who invited me to go to Bosnia with the KCP, introduced me to the interviewees, and encouraged me at every stage of this project. Olivia Dreier, current director of the KCP, taught me about peacebuilding on the ground, which she practiced with grace and kindness as we traveled through Bosnia and Croatia.

I thank Andy Canale, Brita Gill-Austern, and Robert Jonas, my first writers' group, who slowly initiated me into claiming authorship of my own words and ideas, and were the first to hear the pages of this book. I thank my three brothers: Tim, TG, and Dan Snyder. Tim and Dan accompanied me to Bosnia once each. Dan was a huge help with the technological, emotional, spiritual, and philosophical aspects of my initial immersion into these stories, and on my last trip, Tim filmed the interviews, made friends easily with the Bosnian men, and got us invited into households I never could have visited without him. I can't thank my brothers enough for their love, support, truth-telling, wisdom, and strength, supporting their sister with generosity of spirit.

A variety of other friends, colleagues, and mentors contributed immeasurably to this book, each in their own way. I thank Muriel McMahon for her insights about nettles and especially for her seeing the connection between the ritual our Bosnian clinicians did around the rape of the Muslim clients and their babies, and the fact that this ritual actually reversed the polarization that reigns so horribly in our world: namely the "we/they" syndrome; "they're" the "bad ones," "they're" the enemies; we're the good ones; in their case, with the Serbs being the "bad ones" and the Bosnians the "good ones." The creativity group of Jim and Iris Grant and David Hart, my husband of thirty years, supported me during various stages of writing this book. Lissa Sivvy, young enough to be my daughter and wise enough to be a mentor, first recognized the importance of having a chapter on the history of Bosnia. Our Self-Ordination group, a twenty-five-year-"old" group of women, has been one of my centerposts as we've each endured the challenges of life and aging. Thank you Olivia Hoblitzelle, Louise Cochran, Ilona O'Connor, and Ann Dunlap for your faithful support. Polly Young-Eisendrath, Jungian analyst and dear friend, encouraged me through this whole process grounded in her own work on the psychology of conflict.

I thank Anne Yeomans, who invited me to present the material from this book at two conferences in St. Petersburg, Russia, and Loralee Scott, who invited me to be keynote presenter at Seeing Red conferences in Connecticut, and later to be on Seeing Red's faculty, affording me the opportunity to try out ideas on this highly educated, sensitive audience. Thanks to Loralee, too, for listening to my thoughts throughout the evolution of this book, and for suggesting some of the quotes from C.G. Jung. I also thank Sue Ramá for her inspired help as web designer of https://demariswehr.com. My profound thanks to Eleanor Johnson, dear friend and artiste extraordinaire, who made the videos for my website.

Suzanne Kingsbury, my first editor, is an *inspiratrice par excellence,* always encouraging the artist in the author. Along with my writers' group, Suzanne was the first to "hear me to speech" about the book and identify its central theme, the centerpost. Arnie Kotler, my second editor, is a humble man with a depth and breadth of political and spiritual perspectives. His patience and ability to regroup and recatch the theme have been steadying during this challenging journey. Suzanne and Arnie are both midwives of the soul. Without them, this book would not have been born.

The following institutions invited me to present lectures and workshops along the way, allowing me to refine the stories shared in *Making It Through:* Santa Fe Jung Institute; Tucson Friends of Jung; Swannanoa Valley Friends Meeting in Black Mountain, North Carolina; Hanover (New Hampshire) Friends Meeting; the Oak Bluffs and Vineyard Haven Libraries on Martha's Vineyard; the Harmony Institute, St. Petersburg, Russia; the Chautauqua Institution, Chautauqua, New York; and Seeing Red: The Emerging Feminine in Turbulent Times (The Sophia Center, Whispering Pines, North Carolina).

I thank you all from the bottom of my heart.

# About the Author

Demaris Wehr, Photo © Eleanor Johnson (2019)

Demaris S. Wehr PhD has had a lifelong interest in peacebuilding, starting with her Quaker background. She taught religion and psychology at Swarthmore College, Harvard Divinity School, and Episcopal Divinity School. She later became a Jungian psychotherapist, conference speaker, workshop leader, and peacebuilder. Currently on the faculty of The Sophia Center for Transformative Learning, an online graduate school based in Jungian thought, gender studies, and transformative learning, Demaris gives lectures and leads workshops at home and abroad. She lives in Hanover, New Hampshire with her Maine coon cat. For more information, visit www.demariswehr.com

CPSIA information can be obtained
at www.ICGtesting.com
Printed in the USA
JSHW011153241020
9033JS00011B/164